# GUITAR

## SWEEP PICKING
## & ARPEGGIOS

To access audio visit:
www.halleonard.com/mylibrary

Enter Code
1438-2555-4477-3952

# JOE STUMP

# BERKLEE PRESS

Editor in Chief: Jonathan Feist
Senior Vice President of Online Learning and Continuing Education/CEO of Berklee Online: Debbie Cavalier
Vice President of Enrollment Marketing and Management: Mike King
Vice President of Online Education: Carin Nuernberg
Editorial Assistants: Emily Jones, Eloise Kelsey
Cover Design: Ranya Karafilly
Cover Photographer: Rogelio Matamoros
Audio Engineer: Francisco Palomo

ISBN 978-0-87639-181-5

Press

1140 Boylston Street
Boston, MA 02215-3693 USA
(617) 747-2146

Visit Berklee Press Online at
**www.berkleepress.com**

Study music online at
**online.berklee.edu**

DISTRIBUTED BY

HAL•LEONARD®
7777 W. BLUEMOUND RD. P.O. BOX 13819
MILWAUKEE, WISCONSIN 53213

Visit Hal Leonard Online
**www.halleonard.com**

Berklee Press, a publishing activity of Berklee College of Music, is a not-for-profit educational publisher.
Available proceeds from the sales of our products are contributed to the scholarship funds of the college.

# CONTENTS

## ABOUT THE AUDIO

 To access the accompanying audio, go to www.halleonard.com/mylibrary and enter the code found on the first page of this book. This will grant you instant access to every example. Examples with accompanying audio are marked with an audio icon.

Additionally, you can see me performing many of the tracks covered in this book on The Official Joe Stump YouTube channel.

### A Note about Tuning

On the recording, I'm tuned down a half step to concert E-flat. To make the notation match the audio, you can either tune down with me, or set your online playback player to transpose the tracks up a half step.

## CHAPTER 1

# Two-String Arpeggios

*Sweep picking* is a term commonly used to describe a way of playing arpeggios. It essentially means playing through an arpeggio using multiple notes in the same stroke, one on each string. When you ascend, you use a downward motion; when you descend, you use an upward motion.

In this chapter, I focus exclusively on two-string arpeggios. It's funny: many of today's younger players are more familiar with larger arpeggio shapes (five/six-string arpeggios) than smaller ones. Meanwhile, back when I first started to play and learn arpeggio shapes/sequences, those larger shapes weren't nearly as common, and the two-string arpeggio was a real staple of every hard rock/metal player's vocabulary. All of the European hard rock/metal masters that influenced me tremendously (Ritchie Blackmore, Uli Jon Roth, Michael Schenker, Gary Moore, and later on Yngwie Malmsteen) predominantly used smaller two- and three-string arpeggios. It wasn't until Yngwie and then Michael Angelo Batio (in my opinion, two of the founding fathers of shred) that the larger shapes became more prominent.

Figure 1.1 is what I refer to as the first arpeggio in the history of metal. This arpeggio outlines an E minor triad, and the root of the arpeggio is located on the second string. When learning or practicing any arpeggio, always identify its root and chord quality—major/minor/diminished/augmented, etc. Also essential is the note value. Is it a triplet, sixteenth-note figure, sixteenth-note triplet, etc.? Then, you can practice the arpeggio in time with either a metronome or a drum groove.

Figure 1.1 is a triplet: three notes on the beat. This E minor triad is executed by playing a down stroke then a pull-off, then another down stroke. When played correctly and at a faster speed, you'll notice the slight sweeping motion with your pick hand. Note: It's extremely important to pay strict attention to the pick strokes, as they're essential to playing all of the arpeggios in the most efficient way. It's also the best way to be able to execute the arpeggios at faster tempos.

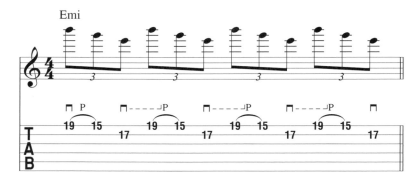

**FIG. 1.1.** E Minor

Figure 1.2 is an A minor triad. It's the same *inversion* (order of arpeggio notes) and rhythmic value as figure 1.1 (triplet). However, the picking pattern is different. Here, you start with a down stroke, another down, and then when you get to two notes on a string, you change your pick stroke and play an up stroke. In this example, the sweep picking motion is even more evident. In my opinion, the logical way to start developing strong sweep-picking technique is to start as I'm doing here, with smaller two-string shapes. Then, keep building and increasing the number of strings involved in the arpeggio shape.

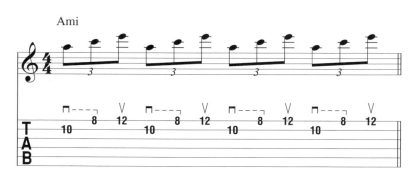

**FIG. 1.2.** A Minor Triad

The third example is another minor triad with the root on the second string. This time, I'm changing the rhythmic pattern to sixteenth notes (pretty much the sixteenth-note equivalent of figure 1.2). The picking pattern is up/pull off/ down/down. Once again, the sweeping type motion is essential in executing this example correctly. The proper picking patterns enable you to play the shapes in the most efficient way. They also sound the best, and what sounds good is always the bottom line.

Also practice this example by turning it around and starting on the second string. It will be the exact same picking pattern, just in reverse: down/down/ up/pull off. Sometimes, reversing the picking pattern and starting the arpeggio on a different string helps internalize it faster and makes playing it easier.

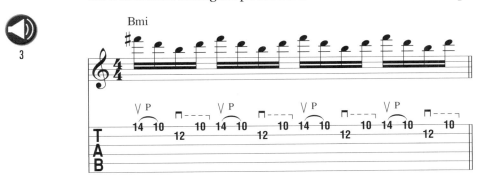

**FIG. 1.3.** B Minor: Sixteenth Notes

Here's another short two-string example, this time involving two arpeggios: G minor and F major. Like figure 1.3, it's played in sixteenth notes, and the picking pattern is down/pull off/down stroke. This lick covers two beats, as opposed to the previous examples that were all one-beat figures.

This pattern is essentially figure 1.1 with an additional pull off, thus making it four notes on the beat instead of a triplet figure. The basic picking pattern is almost identical. Once you get a few of these two-string sweeping patterns under your hands, stretching them into different ideas and rhythmic figures becomes fairly easy.

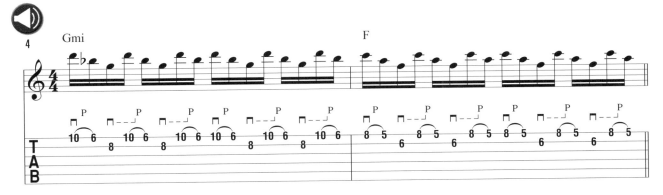

**FIG. 1.4.** Sixteenth Pattern over Two Chords

Figure 1.5 has the arpeggios built from each degree of the E natural minor scale (Aeolian mode) played in two-string sweeps. It's the same picking pattern as figure 1.2. Once again, these are all in root position: the starting note and lowest pitch in the arpeggio is the root.

Later in this chapter, I'll introduce multiple inversions, but these root-position shapes are the easiest ones to execute—a less awkward left-/fretting-hand shape, so you can concentrate on your synchronization, and of course, on the proper picking patterns.

This example is also helpful in that the natural-minor scale is the most commonly used scale in hard rock and metal. Knowing the chords and arpeggios built from each scale tone is extremely useful.

**FIG. 1.5.** E Minor Diatonic Two-String Arpeggios

Figure 1.6 is nearly identical to figure 1.5. However, this time, the diatonic arpeggios for E minor are now played an octave lower on strings 3 and 4 (with the exception of the first E minor arpeggio that's played on the 4th and 5th strings). In bar 7, I added a D♯ diminished arpeggio (borrowed from the E harmonic minor scale) to make it more interesting.

This example is helpful for several reasons. First, your pick hand reacts and feels differently, depending upon the string set you're working on. The other reason is that it's good to be able to recognize these two-string arpeggios on varying string sets in different areas of the neck. Both figures 1.5 and 1.6 are great practice tools, as they cover the arpeggios inside the scale while moving up the length of the fretboard.

**FIG. 1.6.** Arpeggio Practice

Now, finally, here's a musical example utilizing two-string sweeps. This one's key is a combination of A natural and harmonic minor. Once again, all the arpeggios are in root position. Like figure 1.6, it is played on strings 3 and 4. This chord sequence is very classically influenced with the addition of the extra diminished arpeggios. It's an excerpt from my track "Psycho Shred Suite" (first movement) from my 2004 release *Speed Metal Messiah*. A live version can also be found on *2001 A Shred Odyssey*.

The picking pattern is the same as figures 1.2, 1.5, and 1.6.

Throughout the book, I'll be featuring quite a few musical examples using multiple inversions and string combinations, as they're far more fun and rewarding to practice.

**FIG. 1.7.** "Psycho Shred Suite" Excerpt

Figure 1.8 has arpeggios built from each degree of the harmonic minor scale. Note the addition of the augmented chord (1,3,♯5). Also, instead of being in root position, these all start on the 3 of the arpeggio, with the root note being in the middle. This is the second inversion of the chord: from bottom to top, (5,1,3). The fret hand shapes for second inversion chords are slightly more difficult to execute, and you might find a few of them awkward, at first. I'm utilizing the same sixteenth note picking pattern previously found in figure 1.4.

The harmonic minor scale is another scale very common to hard rock and metal. Knowing the combination of triads/arpeggios built from each scale tone is great for creating both chord and arpeggio sequences.

**FIG. 1.8.** Harmonic Minor and Second Inversion

In figure 1.9, we have another musical example, this time in the key of G minor/harmonic minor. In hard rock and metal, it's common to combine the chords of both scales. The picking pattern in the first four bars is the same as figure 1.4: down/pull/down. However, starting in bar 5, on the E-flat major arpeggio, I introduce a new variation: a sixteenth note take on figure 1.2, using that down/down/up sweeping pattern. That pattern stays constant through the last four bars of the example.

In all of these examples, the chord names are all written above each arpeggio. As you're learning them, try to commit the names and shapes on the fretboard to memory. Far too many beginning players only learn the shapes and how to execute them, without having any idea of what they're playing. Don't do that.

FIG. 1.9. Combining G Natural and Harmonic Minor

Figure 1.10 is an old-school metal arpeggio sequence using (as I called it before) the first arpeggio in the history of metal. The picking pattern is from the very first example: down/pull/down. This time, it's six notes on the beat as opposed to the triplet figure in figure 1.1. This one, once again, is in the combination of natural and harmonic minor in the key of E.

Depending on the arpeggio shape and speed I'm playing it at, sometimes I'll anchor my fret hand on the notes of the arpeggio shape and utilize palm muting. You should be able to hear this if you listen closely to the audio clips of each example.

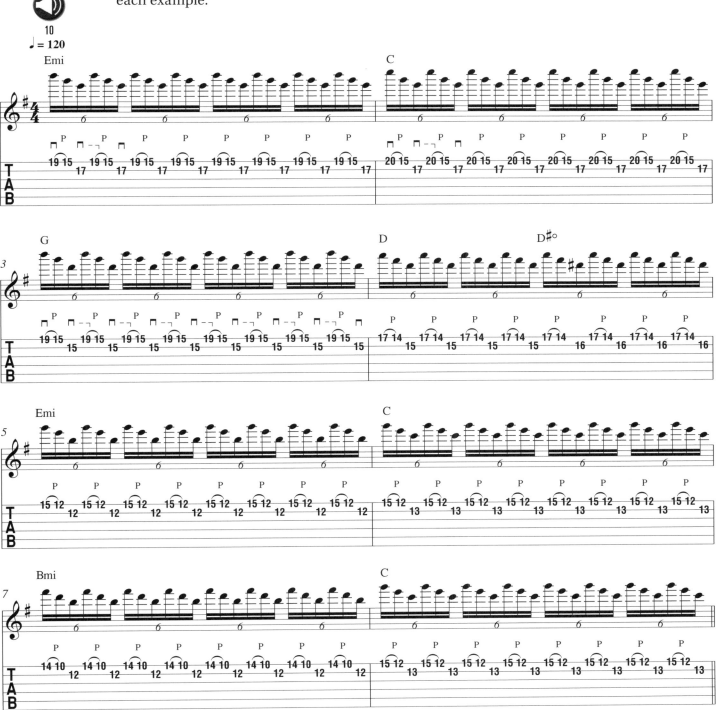

**FIG. 1.10.** Six on a Beat

The musical example in figure 1.11 is by far the most technically demanding one I've covered so far. The picking pattern is constant sixteenth notes (pattern from figure 1.3). The tempo marking for all these exercises are at the speeds I am comfortable playing them, but it goes without saying that you should practice and play them at speeds where you are in control and can command.

Figure 1.11 is a very classically influenced arpeggio sequence moving through a variety of chord types and inversions, combining A natural and harmonic minor. The only non-diatonic arpeggios are the A major/A7 in bar 5 (a dominant sound moving to the D minor chord) and the ♭2 B♭ major chord in bar 10 (very common chord contained in classical music). Also note that in bars 5 and 7 (first two beats of each measure), I'm using the ♭7 of both the A and G major arpeggios, giving it a dominant 7/diminished flavor. Also in bars 6 and 8 on the C major and D minor arpeggios, additional notes from the scale make the arpeggio sequence more melodic and interesting.

The example concludes with a vicious open-string harmonic lick that's guaranteed to work your pick hand. Another challenging aspect of figure 1.11 is the fact that you're playing constant sixteenth notes at a fast clip for a fairly lengthy time period. It will take a certain amount of technical endurance to execute this one cleanly and evenly.

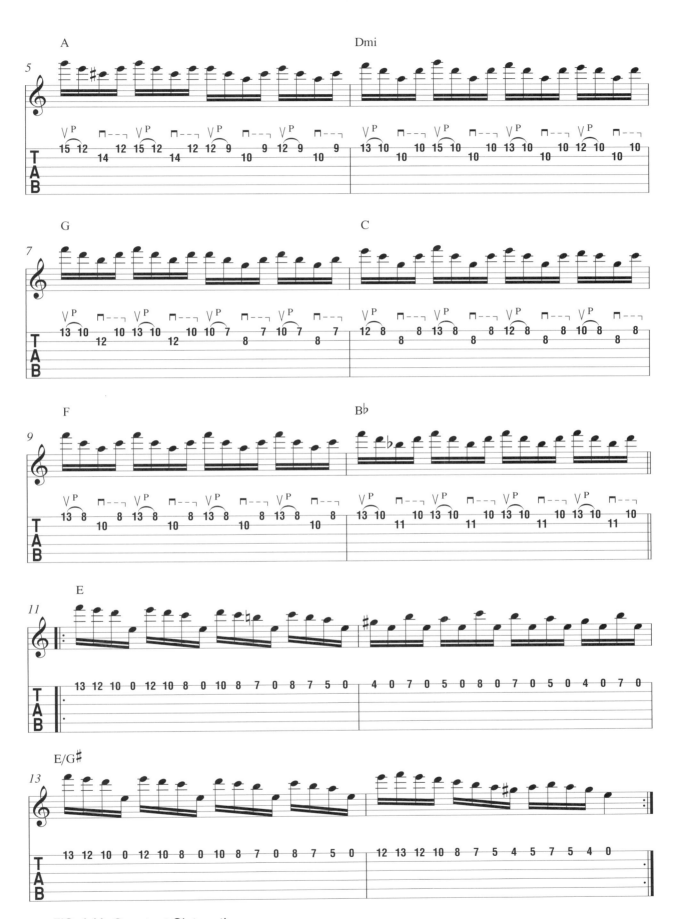

**FIG. 1.11.** Constant Sixteenths

## CHAPTER 2

# Three-String Arpeggios

In chapter 2, I focus on three-string arpeggios. As the shapes get bigger, they start to resemble the chord voicing that they're derived from. Remember the textbook definition of an "arpeggio" is that the chord notes are played individually. If you haven't already, start to make the connection between the arpeggio shape and the basic triadic chord shape it comes from.

Figure 2.1 is a standard three-string sweep, outlining an A minor triad. You should recognize the three-string chord form as the open D minor shape up at the nut of the guitar. Moving it up with the root on the 10th fret (second string), it becomes A minor.

I initially start the arpeggio on a down stroke, but when repeated, the picking pattern becomes up/pull-off/up/down/down/down.

The basic premise of sweep picking is this: When you're ascending, sweep down; when you're descending, sweep up.

The key point is that when you have two notes on a string, you change your pick stroke. Then the standard practice is to play a pull-off (you can also use an alternate pick stroke).

This exercise is written in sixteenth-note triplets (or "sextuplets," as they're often referred to)—six notes on the beat. But you can practice it in triplets as well.

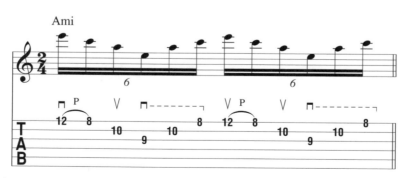

**FIG. 2.1.** Minor Arpeggio on Three Strings

Figure 2.2 is a G major triad arpeggio. It's just the major version of the previous minor shape, which is the basic D major shape from up at the nut of the guitar. This exercise is the same figure as figure 2.1, just reversing the picking pattern and starting the arpeggio on the third string. It's using the same pick strokes as figure 2.1, but backwards: down/down/down/up/pull-off/up.

While figures 2.1 and 2.2 are basically the same (besides the chord type, obviously), you might prefer one over the other. You might have an easier time starting on the third string as opposed to the top string, or vise-versa. Many times, I'll have a three-string arpeggio sequence where I combine both starting points.

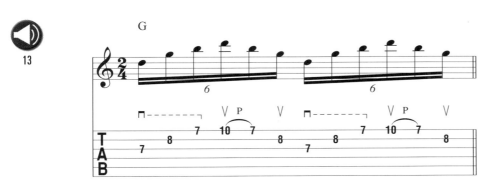

**FIG. 2.2.** Major Arpeggio on Three Strings

In figure 2.3, I add an additional pull-off to the three-string shape and change the note value from sextuplets to straight sixteenth notes. This three-string example spans two beats; the previous examples were just one-beat figures. As I said before, you can take the same shapes, and by using slight variations, change the note value.

The picking execution of the three-string sweep is the same, just with an added extra pull-off. Pay strict attention to the picking patterns shown.

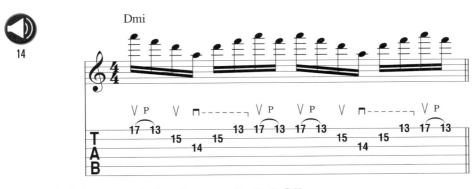

**FIG. 2.3.** Three-String Sweep with Pull-Off

Another sixteenth-note variation on the three-string sweep, figure 2.4 starts on a down stroke (as usual) but after it is played once and repeated, the picking pattern turns around on the top string on an up stroke. This arpeggio lick covers an entire bar (four beats long). All of these short examples will be featured in a musical context later in the chapter.

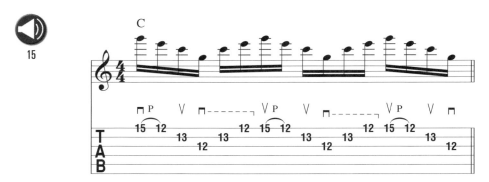

**FIG. 2.4.** Three-String Sweep Picking Variation

This short musical example combines B natural and harmonic minor. It has the basic major and minor shapes featured previously with the addition of a diminished triad in the last two beats of bar 4.

The basic sweeping pattern is like the one in figure 2.1. It's now written in sixteenth note triplets, but you can also practice this one in triplets as well.

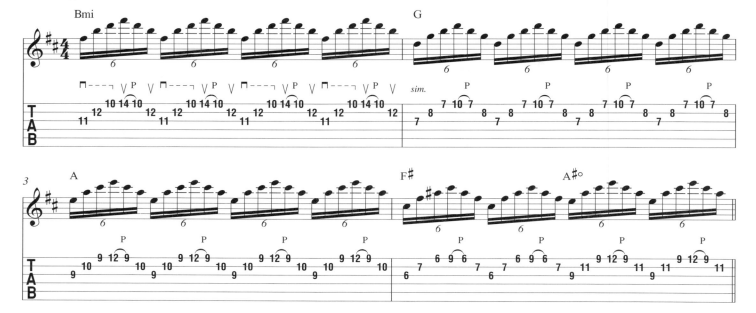

**FIG. 2.5.** B Natural and Harmonic Minor Sextuplet Sweeps

The exercise features diatonic (i.e., within the key/scale) arpeggios for the E natural minor scale. These are like the two-string arpeggios covered in chapter 1, now adding another string. Once again, I'm using those easy-to-play three-string inversions, with the root in the middle of the arpeggio, played on the second string. Again, when playing any arpeggio, it's essential to know its chord type and where the root is.

Like the two-string version in chapter 1, this exercise moves the length of the neck and makes for great practice.

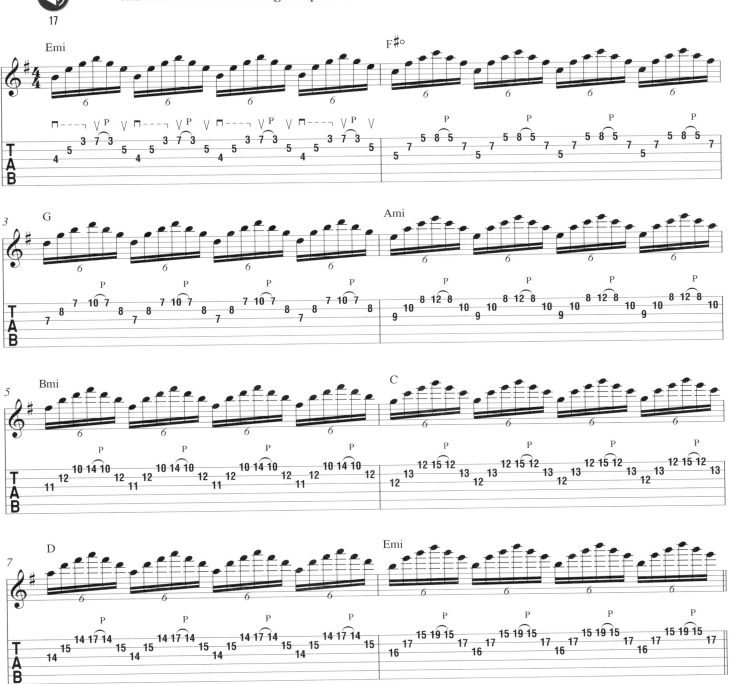

**FIG. 2.6.** E Natural Minor Diatonic Three-String Arpeggios

The next few examples introduce all of the inversions for major, minor, diminished, and augmented three-string arpeggios.

Figure 2.7 is A minor in all of its inversions, moving up the length of the fretboard. I'm playing each of the shapes twice. You might find the first one, using the open high E string, a bit tricky. Also the second shape featured in bar 1, with the three consecutive notes on the fifth fret can be tough as well. For that, I barre my first finger across and use a rolling type of motion to get the proper separation of the notes. I do implement some palm muting while sweep picking; however, I use it more as an articulation control.

The key to playing sweeps cleanly is solely in the proper synchronization between both hands. Also, notice that these A-minor arpeggio shapes are all derived from basic chord shapes you've played a million times.

- The first one is from the open A minor chord at the nut.

- The second one is the top portion of the basic A minor bar chord at the fifth fret with the root on the 6th string.

- The third one is the previously featured open D minor shape and the last one just the top portion of the basic A minor bar chord with the root on the fifth string at the 12th fret.

Again, make the connection between the arpeggio shape and the basic chord shape it comes from. This makes recognizing and internalizing them much easier.

18

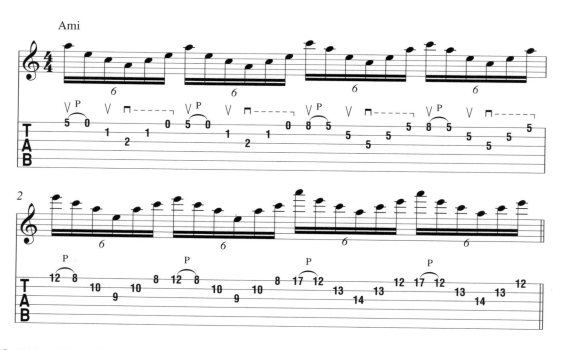

**FIG. 2.7.** A Minor Three-String Sweeps in All Inversions

Figure 2.8 is an E major triad in all of its inversions. Once again, that open one at the nut can be tricky. The second shape featured is just the open basic D major shape, covered previously, while the third one is the top portion of a basic E major barre chord with the root on the fifth string, 7th fret.

For this shape (first E major shape in bar 2), I finger it fourth finger on the 12th fret, first finger (top string 7th fret), and then barre the two notes on the 9th fret with my second finger. The last inversion is just the top portion of the basic E major barre chord with the root of the chord on the 6th string, 12th fret. All of the two- and three-string arpeggios I've covered are basically just the top portion of larger five- and six-string shapes. So I finger the smaller two- and three-string ones just as I would if they were the top portion of a larger shape. That type of fingering consistency is also helpful and essential.

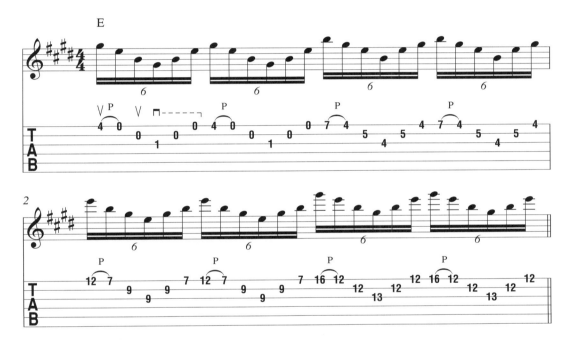

**FIG. 2.8.** E Major Three-String Sweeps in All Inversions

Figure 2.9 is a diminished 7 arpeggio. One cool thing about a diminished 7 arpeggio/chord is that you can name it for any note in the chord, and it automatically inverts itself as it moves up every three frets. It's the same shape, just moving up in minor thirds/three frets.

Depending on the context, I'll finger this one several different ways. One fingering would be (top string to bottom) fingers 4-1-3-4. Another fingering would be 4-1-2-3. Try them both and see what works best for you. The diminished 7 arpeggio is built from the seventh degree of the harmonic minor scale, and it is used quite frequently in metal.

20

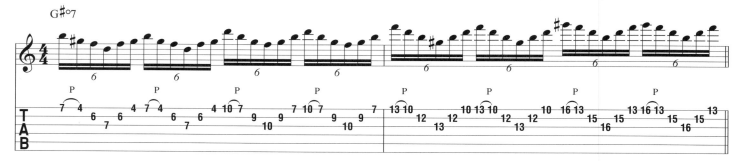

**FIG. 2.9.** G♯°7

Figure 2.10 is a great practice study. Here, we have all of the arpeggios built from the A harmonic minor scale in all inversions. I'm playing each inversion two times using the basic three-string sweeping pattern found in figure 2.1.

We also have the introduction of two new three-string shapes: the mi7♭5 arpeggio built from the second degree of the harmonic minor scale, and the augmented arpeggio. Like diminished 7, the augmented arpeggio inverts by just moving the same shape up the fretboard, this time moving up four frets (in major thirds). Once again, it's very useful info, as the exercise includes all the arpeggio inversions in a scale that's a staple of hard rock and metal.

At the very end, I included a five-string A minor sweep shape. This one's a basic five-string shape starting on the root with two notes on the fifth string and two notes on the top string outlining the basic A minor barre chord at the 12th fret. I start on a down stroke then play a hammer-on. After that, it's consecutive down strokes until I hit the high E string. Then my picking changes to an up stroke to finish out the shape.

21

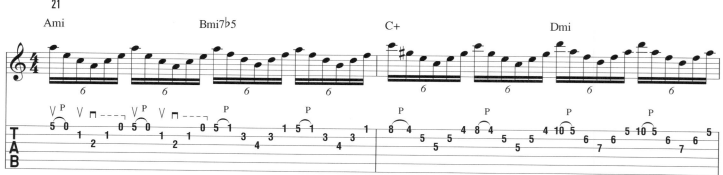

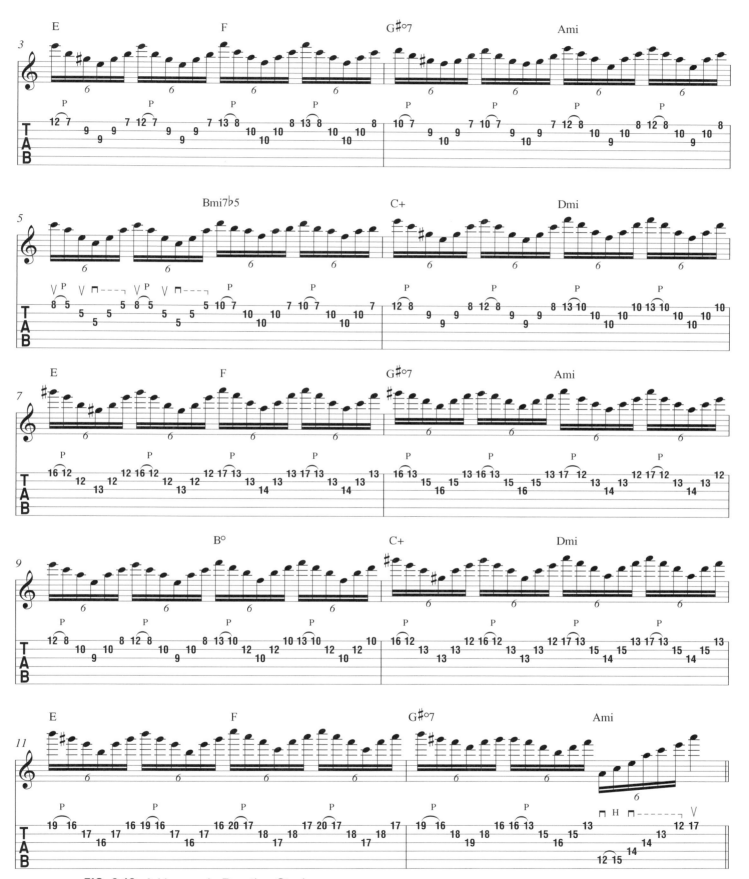

**FIG. 2.10.** A Harmonic Practice Study

Figure 2.11 is a V I study. I'm in A harmonic minor—"the mother of all harmonic minor keys," as I often refer to it—and I'm going from the V chord in the key E major to the I chord, A minor. I'm doing this in all inversions moving up the neck. At the end of the example, I turn the picking around and start the sweep on the third string with consecutive diminished 7 arpeggios and finish up a five-string A minor sweep.

Note: Playing each inversion only once and switching between arpeggios is quite challenging. Start out by practicing each one four times. Then, after that, practice each shape twice, working up to switching inversions on each beat.

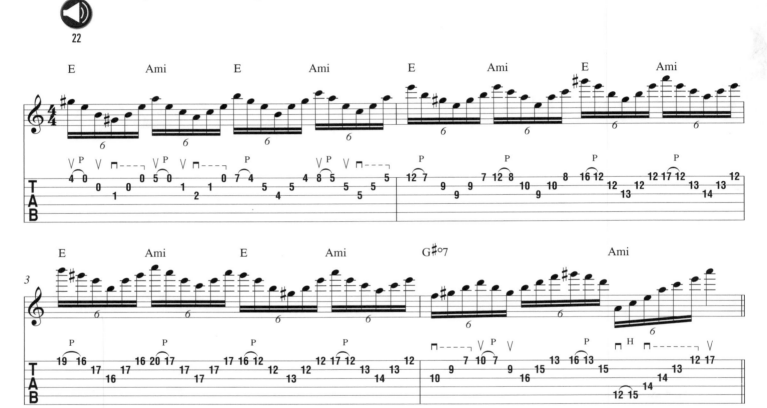

**FIG. 2.11.** V I Inversion Study

Figure 2.12 is another V I inversion study, this time in E harmonic minor moving from B major to E minor arpeggios. Here, I play the B major inversion four times, and then go to two different inversions of the E minor arpeggio (each played twice). That pattern stays constant for the first six bars. In bar 7 each inversion is repeated once. I finish the study once again with some diminished 7 action, then a single-note, harmonic-minor, alternate-picked lick to resolve it.

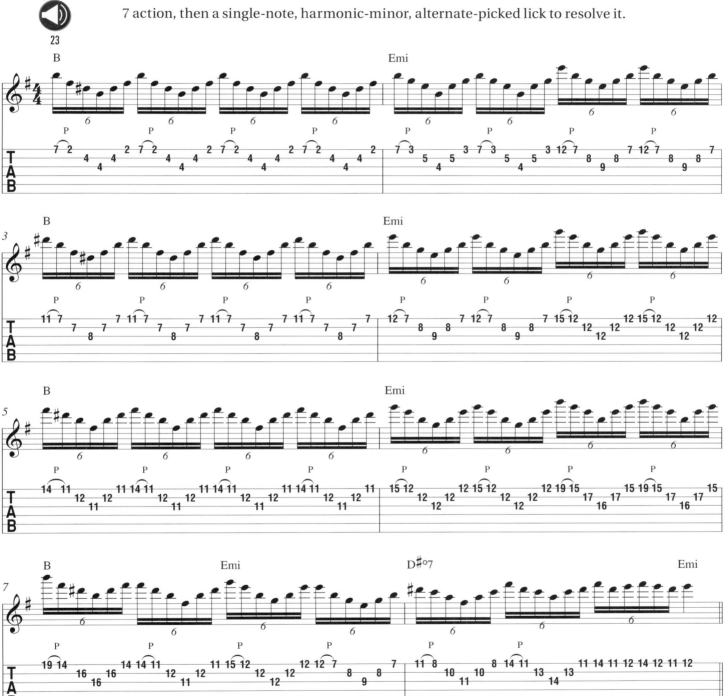

**FIG. 2.12.** Three-String Sweep Sextuplet Study

We conclude with a couple musical examples: something you might hear in the context of a metal track. In figure 2.13, I implement the three-string sixteenth-note pattern previously covered in figure 2.3. For me, this pattern sounds far more complex than it actually is. Also, it sounds killer at faster tempos. The chord sequence is the E natural/harmonic minor combo you've seen quite a bit already. But hey, those are two scales I love to play in, and I use them in my music, so of course they're going to be featured throughout the book!

The sweep sequence is consistent with all of the arpeggios, played four times—with the exception of the C and G major, which are played twice each. I repeat the chord sequence two times, playing all of the arpeggios in each one of its inversions, moving down the neck.

This study is both musical and also helpful for internalizing three-string major and minor arpeggio shapes, in a key commonly used in hard rock and metal.

24

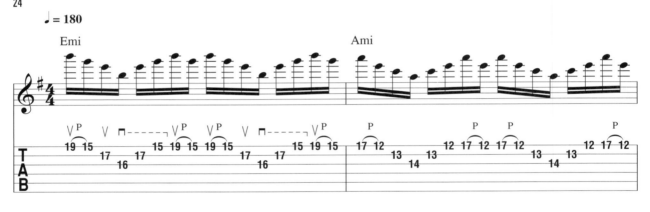

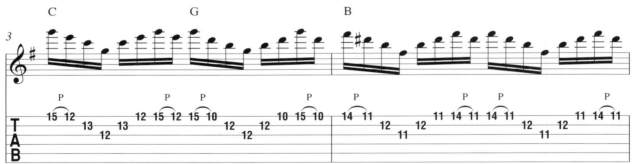

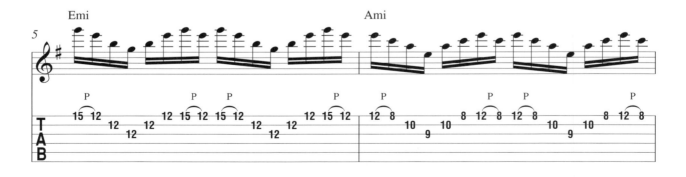

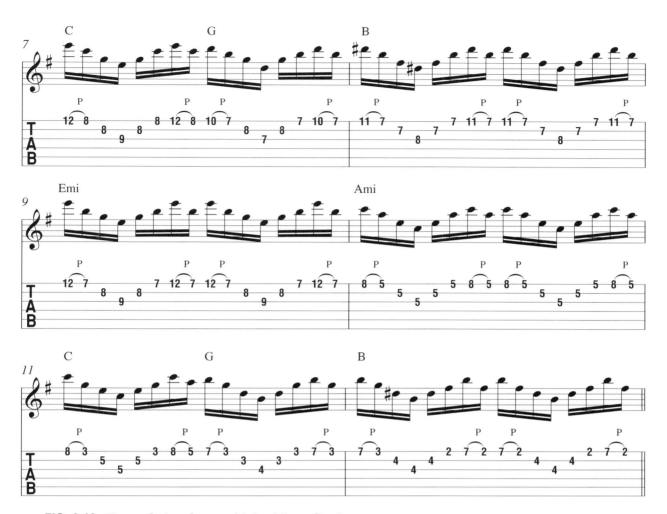

**FIG. 2.13.** Three-String Sweep Major Minor Study

Figure 2.14 is an excerpt from the title track of my 2004 release, *Speed Metal Messiah*. It's in G minor and features a sixteenth-note combination of two- and three-string arpeggio patterns. You should be familiar with the two-string lick used here from chapter 1. The three-string sweeping patterns are the ones seen in figures 2.3 and 2.4.

You can hear that mixing two- and three-string sweeps in an arpeggio section sounds interesting musically; it's quite an effective technique to apply. You can also see that combining sweeping patterns that are all the same note value (in this case, sixteenth notes) is also quite cool. As always, the picking patterns are provided. By this point, you shouldn't need to be reminded to pay strict attention to them.

25

**FIG. 2.14.** "Speed Metal Messiah" Excerpt

## CHAPTER 3

# Arpeggio Studies

Chapter 3 features several arpeggio sections from various tracks of mine. These excerpts illustrate how all of the shorter arpeggios we explored in the first two chapters can be combined and used in a musical context.

The first excerpt is from the first arpeggio section of the track "Chasing the Dragon" from my 2009 release *Virtuosic Vendetta*. The section starts with a sixteenth-note two-string arpeggio sequence that moves up the neck on strings 3 and 4 starting on G major. The section is in the key of A natural/harmonic minor. All of the arpeggios are diatonic to the key with the exception of the A major triad in bar 3. This chord functions as a secondary dominant to the D minor arpeggio that follows it, giving it a classically influenced V I cadence, making it V of IV minor. Also, in bar 7, the D♯ diminished triad serves the same function, resolving to the line that follows in bar 8, which is played over an E major chord.

Another arpeggio of note is in bar 6. Here, I'm adding a B to the C major triad, making it a C major 7 arpeggio. All of the two-string arpeggios in the first eight bars contain the same picking pattern and rhythmic value with the exception of that major 7 arpeggio contained in bar 6, which is played in sixteenth-note triplets. As always, the picking patterns are notated, so pay strict attention.

The next section moves between A minor and E major in three-string sweep shapes. The following two bars repeat the same pattern, except with D minor to A major. In bar 12, you'll see there's a G♯ diminished 7 arpeggio that's played in three strings on the first two beats but then goes to a larger four-string shape in beats 3 and 4 of the measure. I'm using hammer-ons and pull-offs on the larger shape where I have more than one note on a string. Bars 13 and 14 are identical to 9 and 10, with the addition of an A minor five-string sweep in the last two beats of bar 14. The same goes for the following bars in D minor, except the second time around, I go to a different diminished 7 arpeggio. This time, it's D♯ diminished, which sets up the three-string Esus4 arpeggio (the 4 replaces the 3). Esus4 then goes to E major, which V I's (classically influenced resolution/ cadence) to Asus4 to A major. The entire section closes on a five-string A major descending sweep.

# Chasing the Dragon
## 2-3 String Arpeggio, Section 1

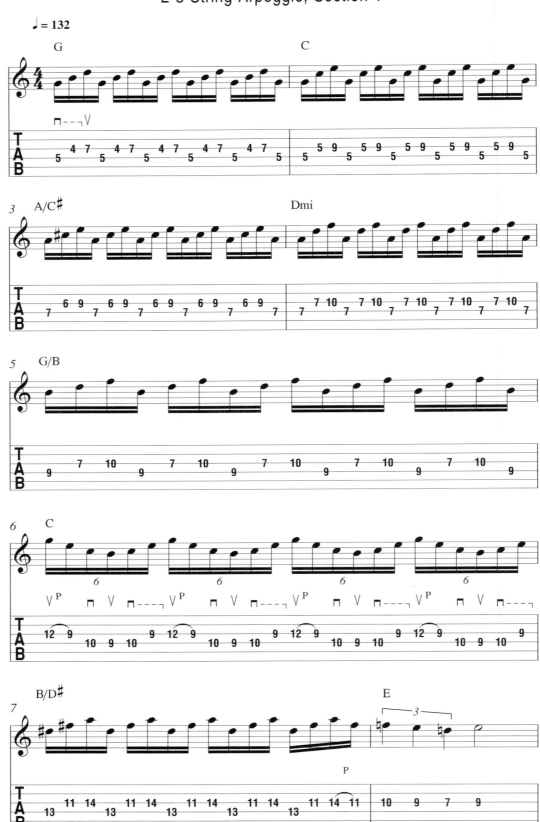

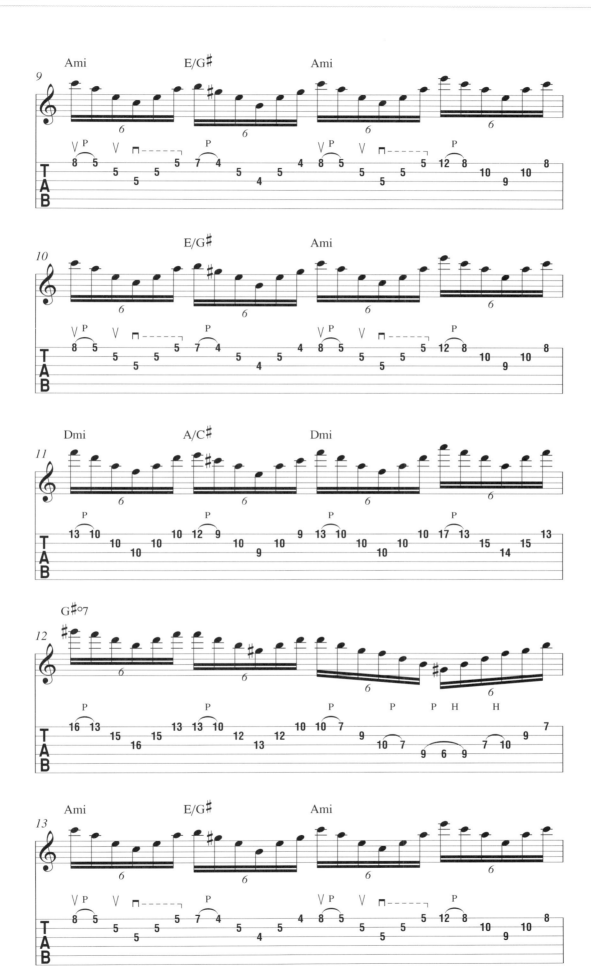

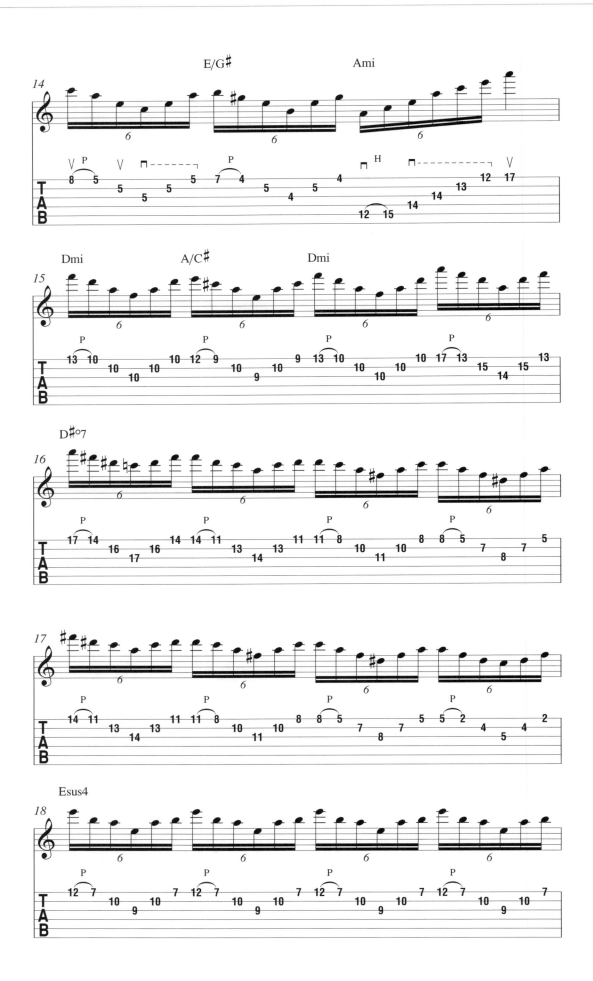

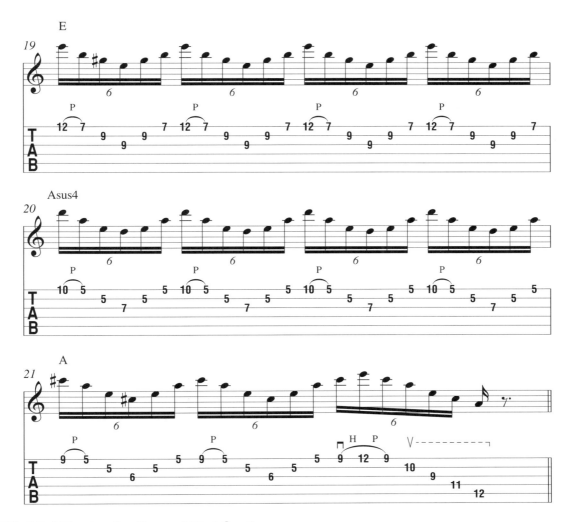

**FIG. 3.1.** "Chasing the Dragon" First Section

The second arpeggio section in the track happens after the main solo section. It starts with a cool, old-school, two-string, sixteenth-note arpeggio pattern on the top two strings, utilizing pull-offs. The first two bars are over A minor, and I'm including additional notes from the scale along with the arpeggio to make it more interesting and melodic. In bar 3, it goes to a two-string F major arpeggio, and the picking pattern changes to a different sixteenth-note variation. That pattern continues in bar 4 as the chords/arpeggios change to E major then two inversions of G♯ diminished 7. The next four bars (5–8) are identical to the first four except playing the next higher voicings of all of the previously played arpeggios. In bars 9–11, it moves to three-string sweeps, all played four times: A minor, F major, to D minor. The section ends with a vicious four-bar blazing harmonic minor run where I utilize a combination of both alternate and economy picking.

# Chasing the Dragon
## 2-3 String Arpeggio, Section 2

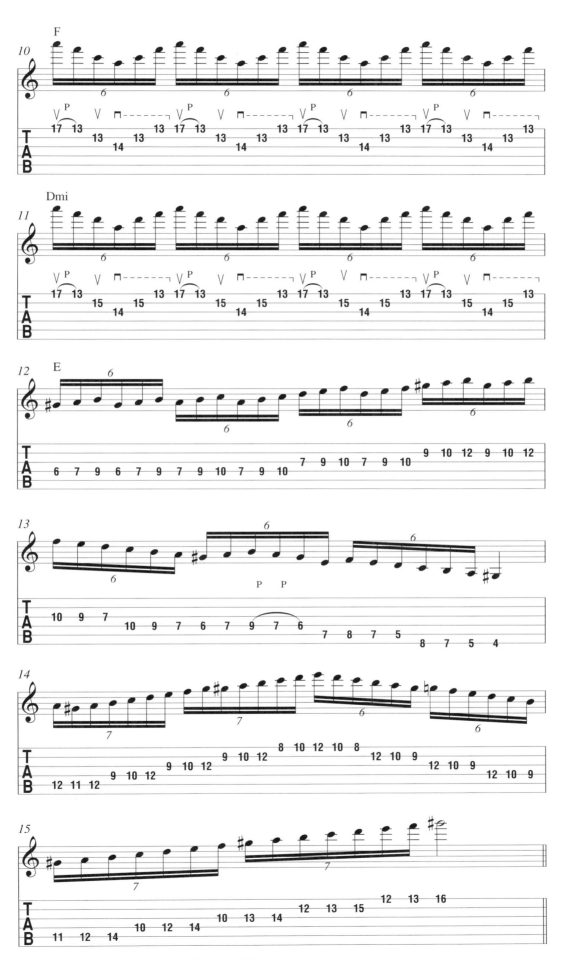

**FIG. 3.2.** "Chasing the Dragon" Second Section

The next example is from the track "Man Your Battlestations" from my 2012 release *Revenge of the Shredlord*. The first eight bars (a repeated four-bar section) are in the key of E minor with the B major chord borrowed from the E harmonic-minor scale. It's a straightforward three-string sweep section, moving through various inversions on the E minor arpeggio, and then adding in the other arpeggios from the scale. One bit you might find a little tricky is the five-note figure on beat 1 of the first three bars. I start the three-string sweep on the third string and add in the leading tone (raised 7th scale tone from harmonic minor) to the E minor triad. Then, I play that same shape starting on the top string with the root replacing the leading tone.

Starting in bar 5, it changes key to A natural/harmonic minor and goes into a descending sequence, playing each one of those inversions two times (with the exception of the D♯ diminished arpeggio, which moves through different inversions/secondary dominant of the V sus/major chord). The following four bars (10–14) are identical to measures 6–9, I'm just playing the same sequence in the next higher set of inversions.

It's all and all pretty straight up, but moving through the different inversions one time apiece (for the first eight bars) is challenging, at a fast tempo.

## Man Your Battlestations

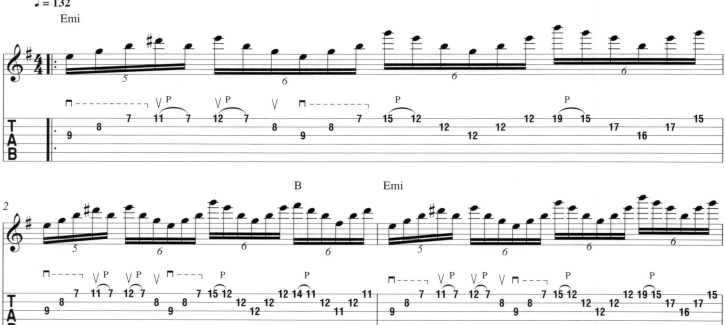

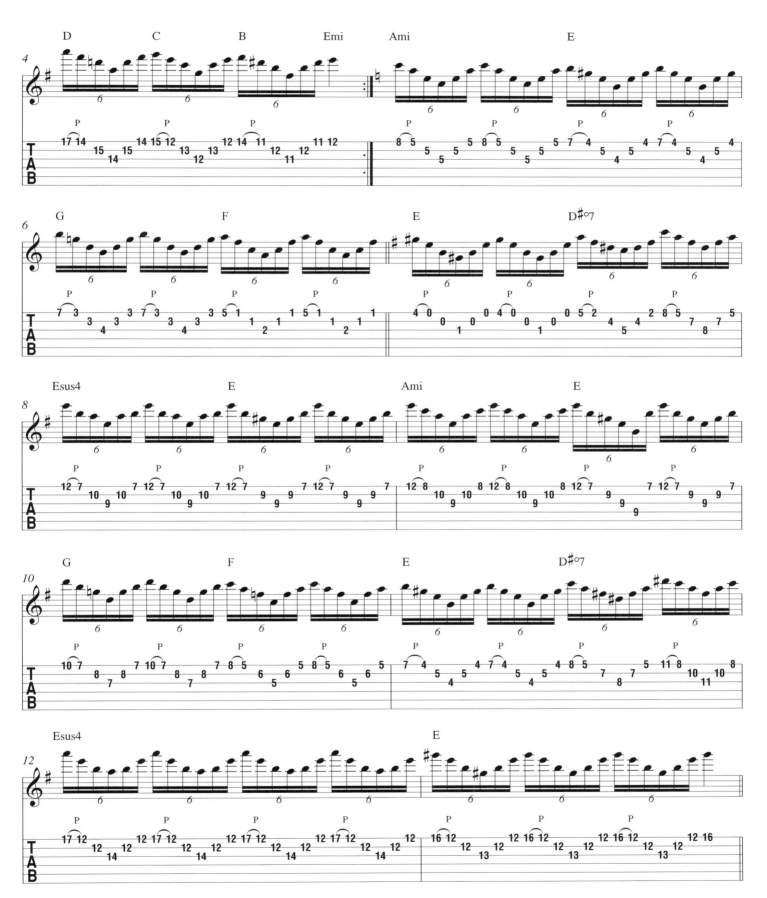

**FIG. 3.3.** "Man Your Battlestations"

Chapter 3 concludes with the arpeggio section from the track "Hostile Takeover" from 2015's *The Dark Lord Rises*. It's a combination of two- and three-string sixteenth-note arpeggio patterns and moves quickly: 212 bpm, in the key of A natural/harmonic minor. The descending two-string section starts with one of the sixteenth sweep-picking patterns covered in chapter 1. (Once again, all pick strokes are notated, so pay attention.) It moves through the chord sequence playing each two-string arpeggio eight times apiece. That remains consistent through the first fourteen bars. Then in bars 15 and 16, I implement a two-string diminished 7 lick with the picking pattern being down/pull-off/ down, followed by a slide that snakes down the neck in minor thirds (three frets at a time). The entire chord sequence then repeats in bars 17–32 in the next lower set of inversions, this time in three-string sweeps. This lick is one of the three-string sixteenth-note patterns featured in chapter 2—a standard three-string sweep execution with a pull-off added to change note value.

This excerpt also represents a compositional technique I often implement during arpeggio sections. I first play the chord sequence using smaller arpeggio shapes. Then, I repeat the identical progression using larger, and many times, more technically challenging/more intense shapes.

32, 33

# Hostile Takeover

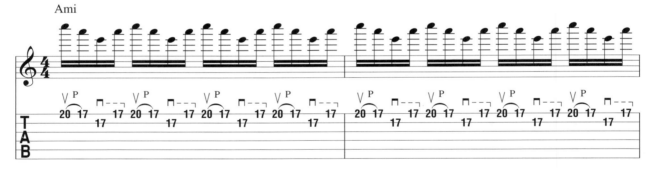

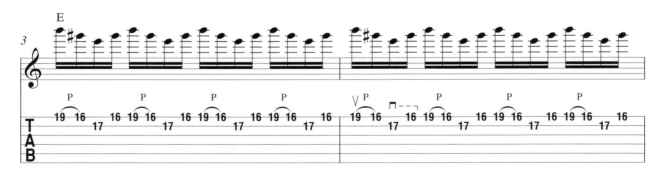

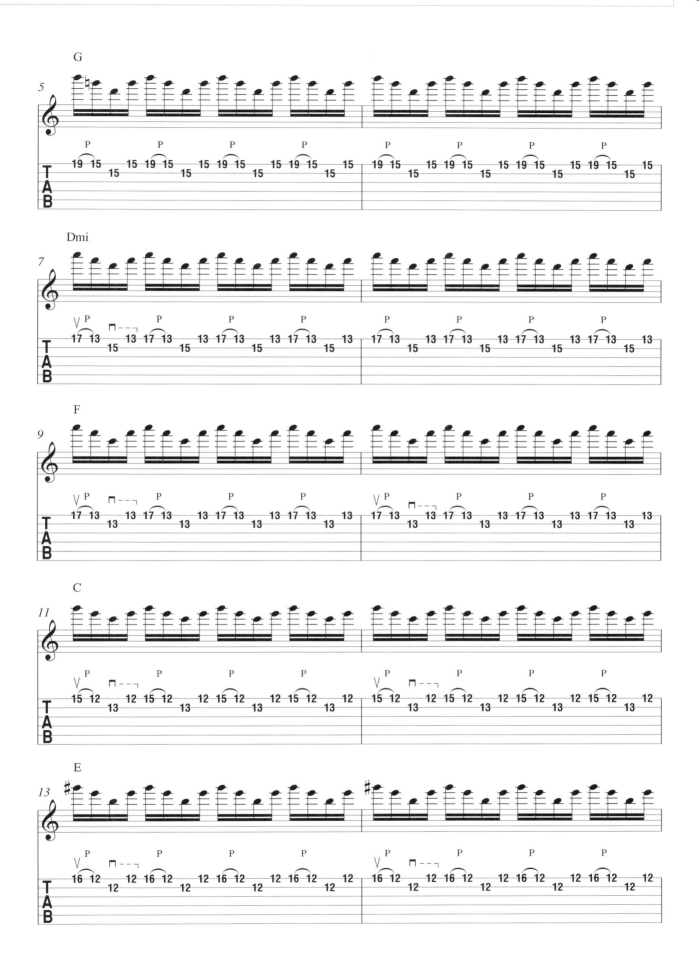

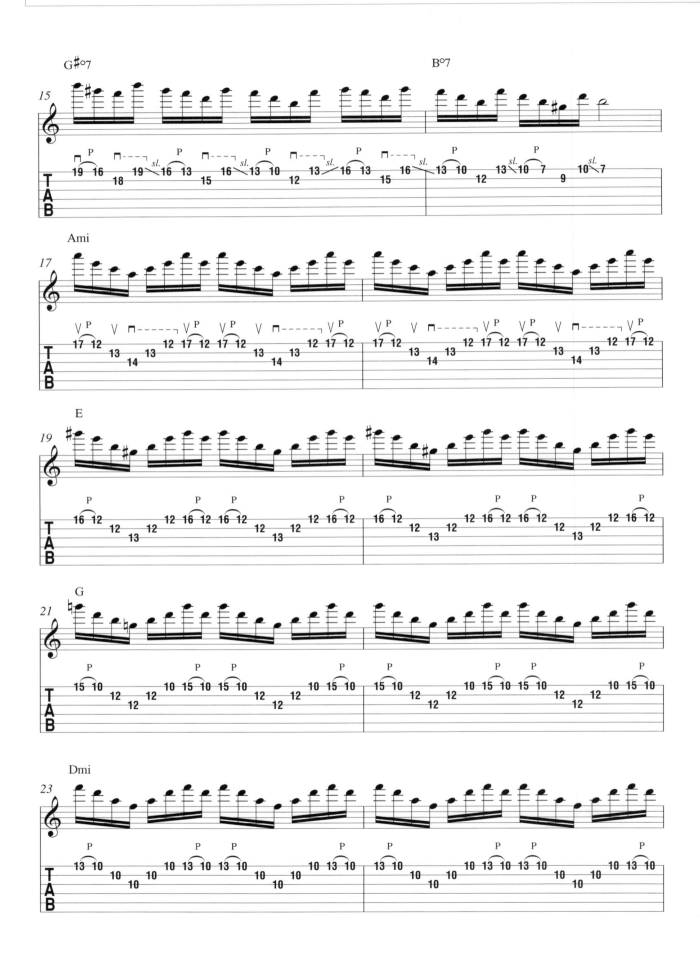

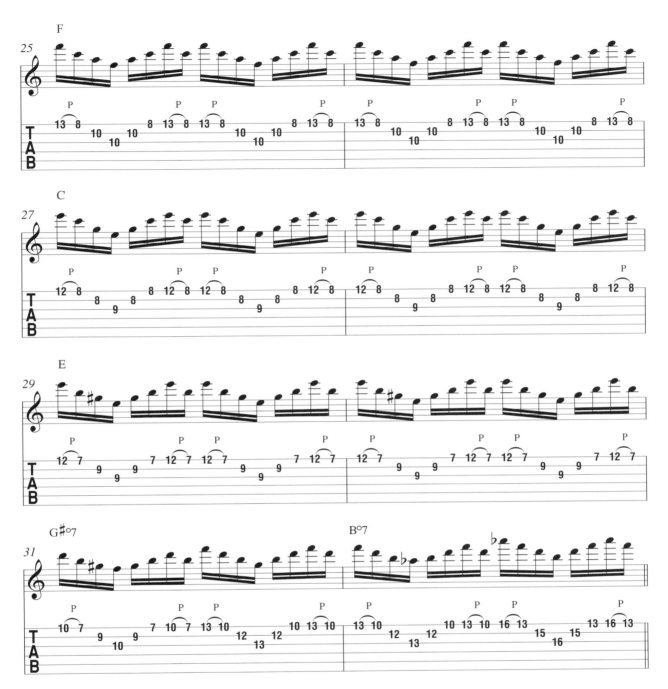

**FIG. 3.4.** "Hostile Takeover"

Hopefully some of these musical examples will inspire you to create your own arpeggio sections/etudes, as playing and practicing in a musical context is what it's all about.

# Four-String Arpeggios

In chapter 4, I'll be covering four-string arpeggio shapes. Many younger players aren't nearly as familiar with four-string arpeggios, compared to the more commonly used three- and five-string shapes. One extremely useful thing about them is that since they're mostly played in an even sixteenth-note rhythm (four notes on the beat), you can combine them with other arpeggio and single-note lines that have the same note value.

Figure 4.1 is a four-string B minor arpeggio. Once again, I'm using the easiest fret-hand shape: the open D minor shape from the nut. The picking pattern is consistent with the basic three-string shape that's been previously covered: all down strokes while ascending. You get to two notes on a string then change your pick stroke to an up, play a pull-off, and then two up-strokes when you descend. The rhythm is straight sixteenth notes (four notes on the beat).

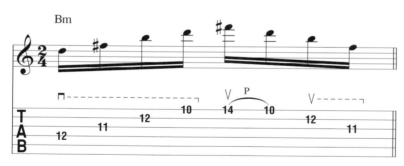

**FIG. 4.1.** B Minor Arpeggio

You might find the major version of this shape a bit easier to play. As you can see, it's just the top four strings of the open C shape from the nut (starting in 7th position, it becomes G major). Notice that the arpeggio root in both shapes is located on the 2nd string.

You can sweep this one, just like the picking pattern in figure 4.1. But I'll also pick four-string shapes by combining alternate and sweep picking, as in figure 4.2. The ascending portion is exactly the same (down/down/down/down), then I play the up stroke, and then down/up/down. I've notated this G major shape with that combined picking pattern. Regardless of how cleanly you play, an alternate-picked line is always going to have a different type of sound than a straight sweep-picked line. While the approach in figure 4.2 is not nearly as common, I use it quite frequently in my playing depending upon which sound I prefer.

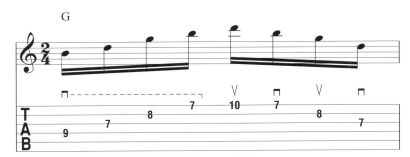

**FIG. 4.2.** G Major Arpeggio

Figure 4.3 is not a four-string sweep shape, it's a three-string A♯ diminished 7 arpeggio. But since it's in a sixteenth-note rhythm, and I often combine it with four-string sweeps, I've included it in this chapter. You can pick it using the combined sweep/alternate pattern that's notated in figure 4.3, or you can try adding hammer-ons and pull-offs to the shape anytime you encounter two notes on a string. Depending on the context and speed at which I'm playing it, I'll pick it in a variety of ways.

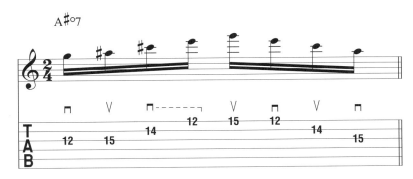

**FIG. 4.3.** A♯ Diminished 7 Arpeggio

A G diminished triad arpeggio, the root remains on the 2nd string and the picking pattern is the same as figure 4.1.

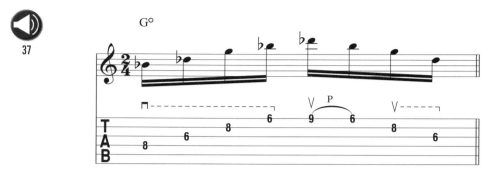

**FIG. 4.4.** G Diminished Triad Arpeggio

Figure 4.5 uses the same E natural minor diatonic arpeggio shapes that were covered previously, utilizing those easiest-to-finger fret-hand inversions. I'm just taking those shapes from chapters 1 and 2, each time adding another string, making the shape larger and sweeping over more strings. I wrote them just once a piece, but you can practice these, repeating each arpeggio multiple times moving up the neck. You can also use either or both of the picking options shown previously.

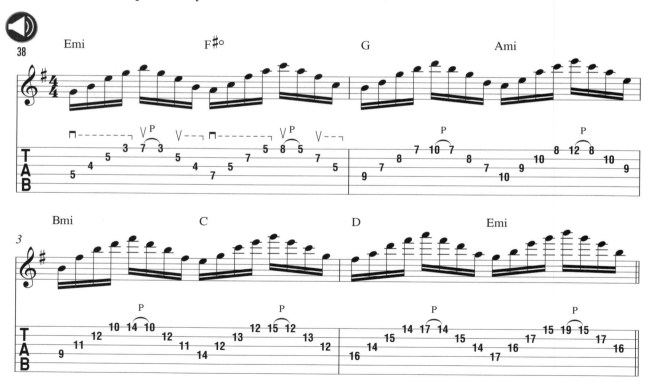

**FIG. 4.5.** Arpeggio Shapes

Figure 4.6 presents E minor in four-string inversions, I'm playing each inversion twice, moving the inversions up the neck. It's important to make the connection between the arpeggio shape and the easy triadic chord shape it's derived from. In measure 1, it's that D minor shape from the nut just moved up. In measure 2, it's the top four strings of the E minor barre chord with the root on the 5th string at the 7th fret and the last inversion just the top portion of the root VI minor barre chord.

**FIG. 4.6.** E Minor Four-String Inversions

Figure 4.7 is the same as figure 4.6, but now, it's G major four-string arpeggio inversions moving up the neck.

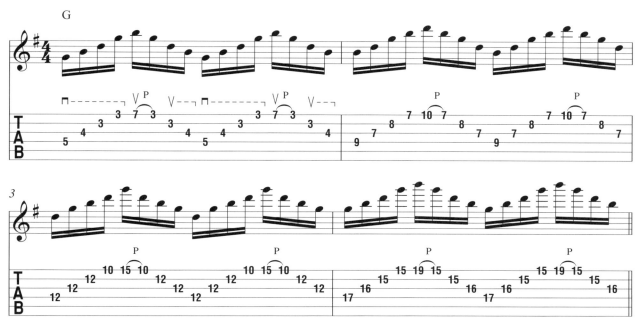

**FIG. 4.7.** G Major Four-String Inversions

Figure 4.8 is a neo-classical four-string sweep study in the combination of A natural/harmonic minor. It starts out with the A minor inversion at the 5th fret played two times. With all the 1st finger barring/rolling involved in executing this shape, I find it comes out more articulately with that combination of alternate and sweep picking I illustrated earlier (just my personal choice). In bar 2, I go to the easier E major shape, and in bar 3, to that three-string previously covered diminished 7 arpeggio (G♯ diminished this time) starting on a down stroke and using a hammer-on to get the second note on the 3rd string to start it.

In the next four bars, I play each arpeggio twice using straight sweep picking, with the exception of the tricky D minor shape (same inversion shape as bar 1) in bar 6. (I use that sweep/alternate combo for that one.) In bar 8 (E major arpeggio), beats 3 and 4, I add in a five-string shape starting on the 3 of the chord, playing two notes on the 5th string and two notes on the top string. As always, the picking pattern is notated below the music.

In bar 9, it goes to a four-string A minor arpeggio, the same shape that started the study except twelve frets/one octave higher. Then, there are four three-string A minor inversions played in sixteenth notes moving down the neck.

The etude ends as E major resolves to A. You can see how the sixteenth-note three-string arpeggios in the last two bars work nicely with all of the previously played four-string shapes, making the entire study interesting to practice as well as very musical.

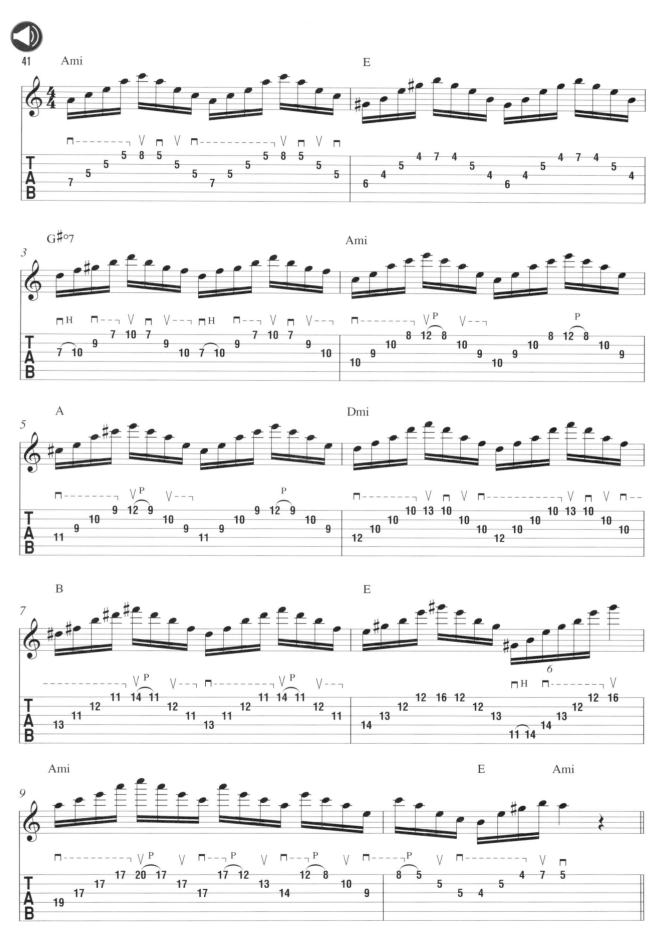

**FIG. 4.8.** Four-String Sweep Study

Figure 4.9 is another classically influenced etude, this time in E minor. I'm very fond of this chord sequence. It sounds very neo-classical even though it's completely diatonic—meaning, it contains none of the additional outside the key arpeggios I've used in previous examples, that were derived from classical harmony.

The descending chord sequence is E minor, B, G, D, A minor, E minor, back to B major resolving to E minor. In each measure, all of the arpeggios are four-string shapes played twice. The only exception is the five-string full E minor sweep shape that finishes the first half of the etude on the last two beats of bar 8. In the second half, the chord sequence just repeats, playing the next lower inversions of all the previous shapes. The only exceptions are the final two bars where, in the second to last bar (bar 15 of the study), I use a three-string diminished 7 arpeggio in *quintuplets* (five notes on the beat).

When played at fast speeds, that diminished figure has a very cool sound, and I use it quite frequently in my music. I execute the shape starting on a down stroke, then I play a hammer-on. After that it's two down strokes and then an up-stroke to finish the five-note pattern. I move that up the neck in minor thirds (three frets at a time), and as you can see, since diminished 7 is symmetrical, it works killer at fast tempos.

The study ends on a single note line in E harmonic minor. The last two beats of the final bar contain a very cool classical arpeggio I use all the time. It's the minor triad with the 2nd degree of the scale added to it. That arpeggio resolves the entire piece nicely giving it a classical violin type of sound.

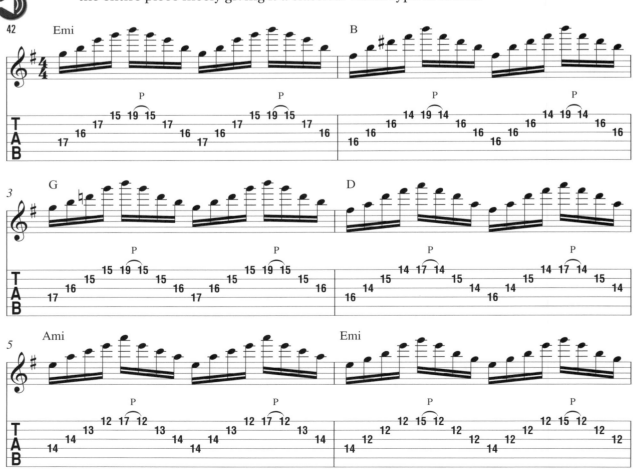

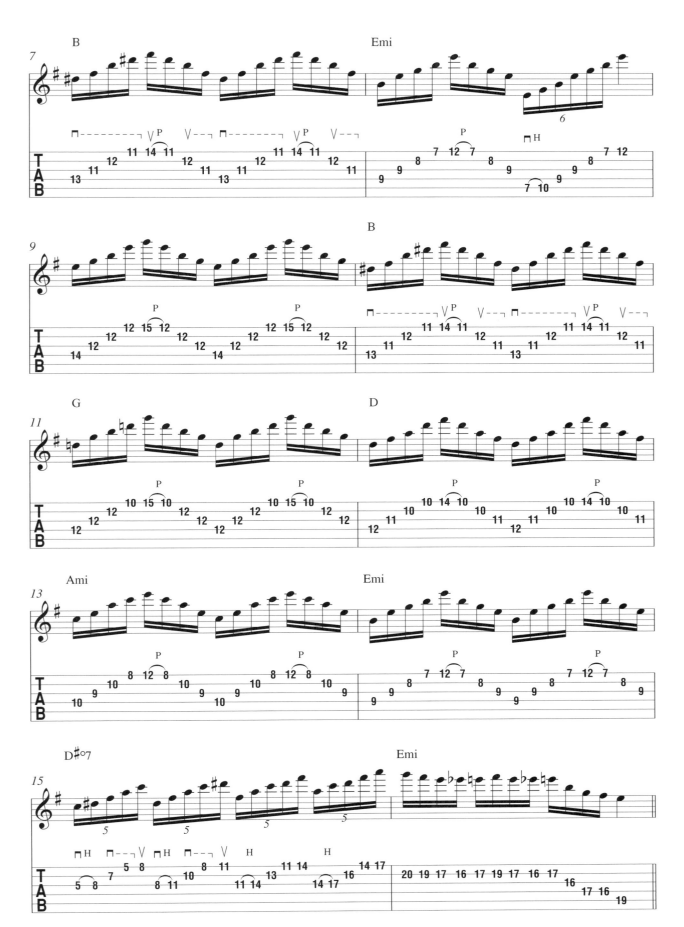

**FIG. 4.9.** E Minor Chord Sequence

**CHAPTER 5**

# Five-String Arpeggios

In chapter 5, we move on to five-string arpeggio shapes. The five-string arpeggio is far and away the most popular among many players. Usually, it's the sound of these bigger/multi-string arpeggios that attract them to sweep picking/arpeggio play to begin with.

Figure 5.1 is a B minor arpeggio. Once again, the first two examples covered here are the two easiest fret-hand shapes (figure 5.1, the larger version of the open D minor shape from the nut, and figure 5.2, the major shape being the open C shape). The picking pattern remains consistent with what we covered previously, sweeping all down strokes until hitting the top string then changing to an up stroke, adding the pull-off, and descending with all up strokes.

The most difficult part of the first three examples is the fact that you're playing a quintuplet: five notes on the beat. Logically speaking, a five-note figure sounds like a cross between four sixteenths and a sextuplet (sixteenth-note triplet). The hardest thing about odd groupings is that the slower you play them, the more awkward they become. However, you just can't come out of the gate blazing these up if you've never played them. Just try to execute the figure evenly and in time, using a metronome, and it will eventually feel more natural.

43

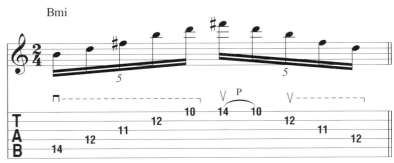

**FIG. 5.1.** B Minor Arpeggio

Figure 5.2 is a G major five-string sweep outlining the open C shape from the nut. This one might even be a little easier to execute than the minor triad in figure 5.1, so you might consider starting with this one when first trying to tackle five-string sweeps. Also note that in the first six examples in this chapter, the root of each arpeggio is on both the 5th and the 2nd strings. When playing an arpeggio, it's important to know where the root is, as well as the chord shape it's derived from.

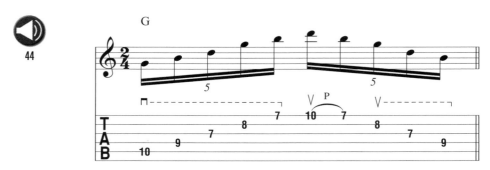

**FIG. 5.2.** G Major Sweep

Figure 5.3 is the diminished triad version of the standard five-string sweep. You might try several different fret-hand fingerings to see what works best for you. The two standard fingerings are (low to high, 5th string to top string) 4-3-1-3-1-4 and 4-2-1-2-1-3. I myself use the first fingering, but some players will play that shape in either or a combination of those two standard fingerings.

Practice all these shapes through the diatonic arpeggios in the E natural minor scale, and/or create your own chord sequences and etudes.

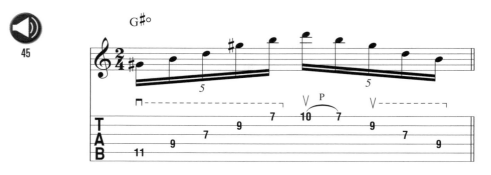

**FIG. 5.3.** G Diminished Triad Sweep

Figure 5.4 is the same five-string minor shape as in figure 5.1 (except this time it's A minor). This time, I'm changing the note value from a quintuplet/ five-note grouping to a sextuplet by adding a hammer-on and pull-off to the top of the shape. This is one of my favorite five-string patterns and I use it often. Also, by changing the note value to an even figure (six notes as opposed to five), you can now subdivide the arpeggio shape and practice it in either triplets or sixteenth-note triplets.

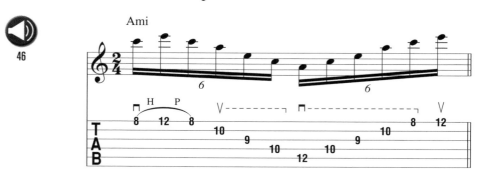

**FIG. 5.4.** A Minor Arpeggio

An F major arpeggio utilizing the same triplet/sextuplet pattern as the previous example, figure 5.5 is just the major version of figure 5.4, or the open C shape derived from the nut. The picking pattern is identical to the A minor in figure 5.4. Like all the other featured shapes, you can practice it diatonically through a scale or try combining it with other arpeggios of the same note value to create your own arpeggio sections.

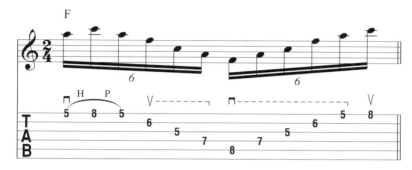

**FIG. 5.5.** F Major Arpeggio

This particular five-string pattern has been shown several times in previous chapters. Now, I'm using it with a diminished triad. All I'm doing is taking the five-string diminished shape from figure 5.3 and adding a second note on the 5th string (in this case, it's the 5th of the triad).

This fingering involves what might be a significant stretch for your fretting hand. I start the arpeggio on a down stroke, then play a hammer-on, and after that, it's all consecutive downs until I hit the second note on the top string. Then following suit with everything I've done previously, I change my pick stroke to an up, play a pull-off, and then continue with all up strokes. Since it's an even grouping, you can practice this one as a triplet or sixteenth-note triplet (sextuplet).

Another picking I'll do with all of these five-string shapes is sweep-pick them ascending and then alternate-pick them descending. There's a distinct difference in the sound, and how I pick them really depends upon the context of the track and the speed I'm playing them.

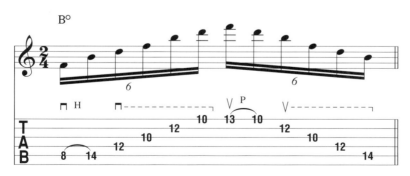

**FIG. 5.6.** B Diminished Arpeggio

Figure 5.7 includes all of the five-string inversions of E major, moving up the neck. With all of these shapes, there are always two notes on the 5th string and two notes on the top string, making the picking pattern identical for all of them (as notated).

With the larger triadic shapes, it's easier to see what chord voicing each arpeggio is derived from. The first one starts on the root of the triad and comes from the standard major barre chord with the root of the triad on the 5th string. The second arpeggio is a first inversion, starting on the 3rd of the triad coming from the root 6 major barre chord. The last one is an E major in second inversion, starting on the 5th, derived from the open C shape.

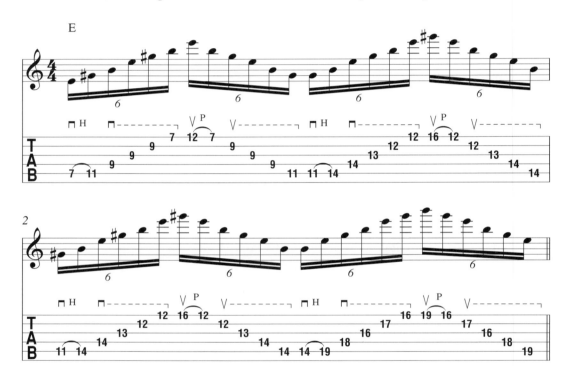

**FIG. 5.7.** E Major Five-String Inversions

Figure 5.8 includes all the inversions of the D minor triad. Identical in order to the previous major example, it starts on the root, then 3rd, then 5th moving up the neck. All of these shapes once again have two notes on the 5th string and two notes on the top string. The picking pattern remains the same.

One thing you might have trouble with is the second D minor shape that starts on the 3rd of the triad (first inversion). I play that one with my 1st finger, then barre the notes on the 4th and 5th strings with my 3rd finger, and then play the rest with my 1st finger. With all of that barring, it'll take a fair amount of work to get clean.

I've also included an alternate fingering in the following measure, moving the 3rd of the arpeggio F to the 6th string. I'll play either of those fingerings depending upon the speed and the context of how I'm using that particular shape.

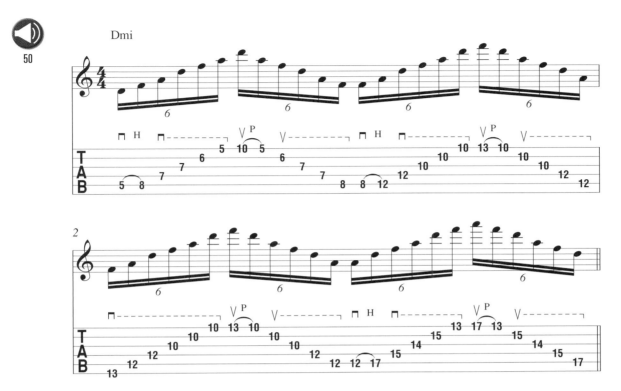

**FIG. 5.8.** D Minor Triad Inversions

Figure 5.9 is an E natural/harmonic minor chord sequence utilizing the five-note/quintuplet pattern shown in figures 5.1 and 5.2. I kept it really simple, using just the two basic major and minor shapes.

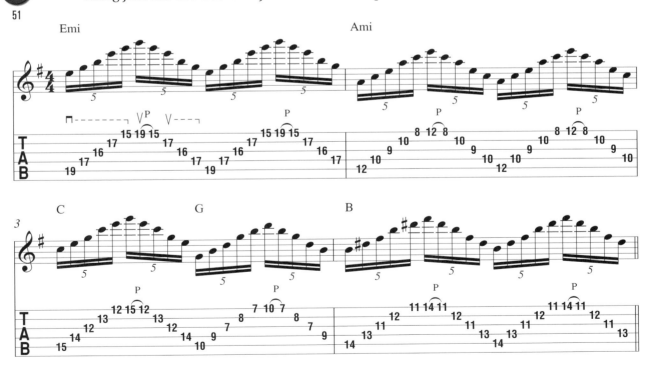

**FIG. 5.9.** E Natural/Harmonic Minor Chord Sequence

A chord sequence in B natural/harmonic minor, this one starts with that five-string triplet/sextuplet picking pattern shown in figure 5.4. The first time through the arpeggio sequence, I start with those easy-to-play minor/major/

diminished inversions. Then the second time through I add another inversion shape and do what's called a *figure 8*, where I'm descending from one inversion and linking it to another. In the 5th bar of the example, I start out descending from that first minor shape. Then, shifting my fret-hand, I play the root of the arpeggio on the first note of beat 2 with my 1st finger. I then play through that shape and finish the measure off by shifting position back, and I start the last sextuplet of the measure with my 4th finger.

All of the rest of the arpeggios in the etude follow the same figure-8 fingering/shifting pattern. The only thing that changes is the chord type. In the last measure, I add a three-string F♯ major sweep after the five-string figure 8 and then end the etude on a C♯ diminished triad.

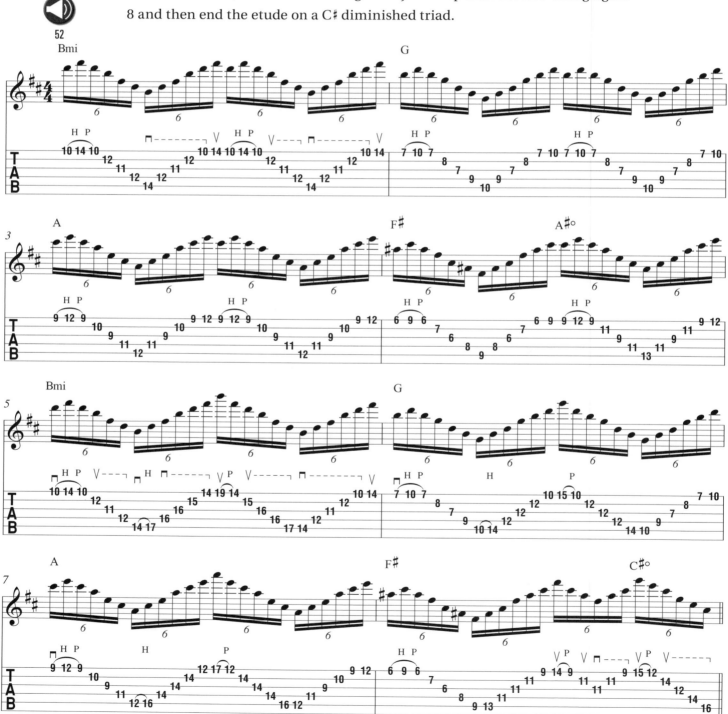

**FIG. 5.10.** B Natural/Harmonic Minor Chord Sequence

Figure 5.11 is a Bach inspired Baroque chord sequence in G minor also used in the classic Deep Purple track "Burn." Anybody familiar with my work knows that Ritchie Blackmore is one of my heroes, and his playing, performing, and composing have impacted me greatly. He was the first guy to use scales like Harmonic, Hungarian minor, dominant Phrygian, and double harmonic minor (what he always referred to as the "snake charmer scale"), and bring things like classically influenced lines and arpeggios to hard rock. I still listen to him religiously and always find his playing inspiring.

The first time through this chord sequence, I keep it quite simple playing one arpeggio shape per measure (with the exception of measures 7 and 8 where I use multiple inversions of D major). All these shapes have been covered previously and all contain that sweeping pattern with two notes on the 5th string and two notes on the top string, making the picking identical for all them.

The second time through, things get quite a bit more intense. The G minor in bar 9 starts with a five-/three-string combination and then moves to that five-string hammer-on pull-off six-note shape. In the following measure on C minor, I reverse the two inversions/sweeping patterns from the previous bar and end the measure on the root.

The same type of five-string/three-string combinations continue in the next three bars over the F, B♭, and E♭ major arpeggios. (Per usual, all of the pick strokes are notated, so *pay attention!*)

In bar 14, over the C minor chord, I use a cool technique I'm really quite fond of, where I'm just blazing through the inversions in seven-note groupings and only playing them ascending. That kind of quick/intense ascending-only sweeping contrasts nicely in the context of the other arpeggio patterns.

The five-string/three-string combinations return in measure 15 over the D chord.

You can see that in the second half of this arpeggio sequence, I'm using all previously covered standard five-string and three-string arpeggios. Really, executing these shapes individually is fairly pedestrian. But the way I'm mixing/matching and combining them makes it far more intense, technically demanding, and of course more interesting musically.

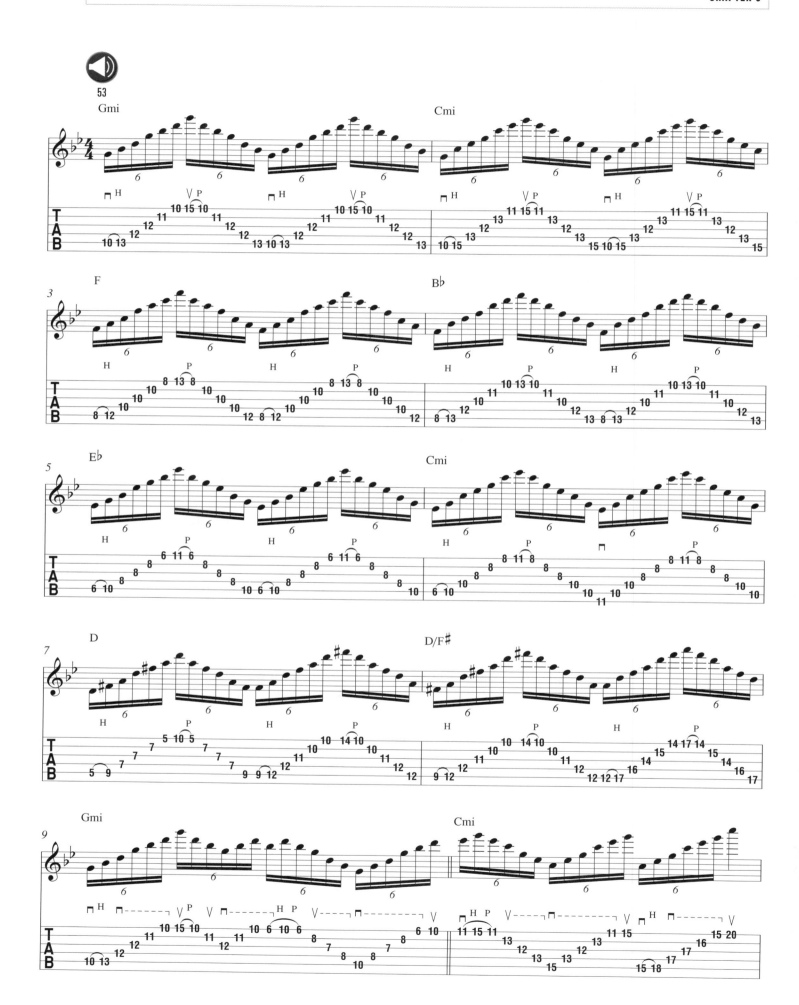

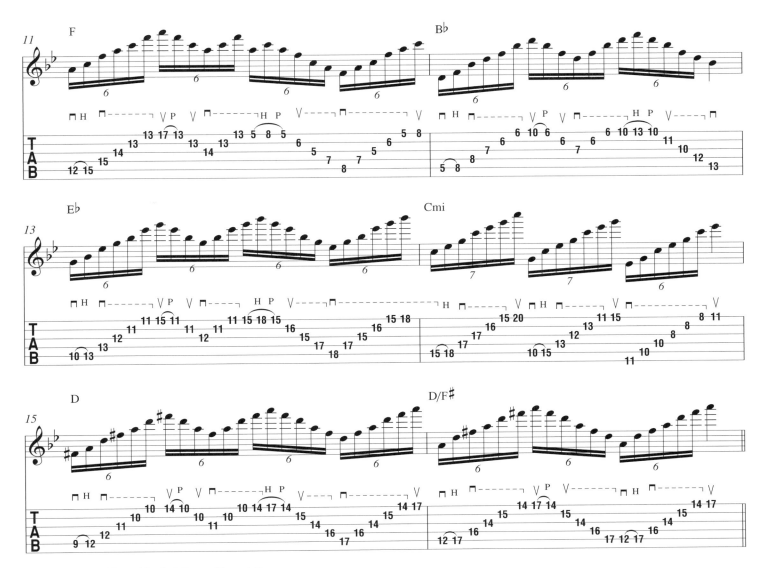

**FIG. 5.11.** G Minor Chord Sequence

## CHAPTER 6

# Prelude, Demon's Eye, and The Dark Lord's Allegro

In this chapter, I'll be covering several arpeggio sections from my various recordings. All of these excerpts contain a combination of multiple arpeggio shapes played on varying string sets.

## "PRELUDE"

This is the opening track/intro to the title track from my 2004 release *Speed Metal Messiah*. It starts out with a combination minor triad and diminished 7th inversions (you should be quite familiar with these three-string inversions, by this point). Alternating between A minor and G♯ diminished 7, I move up the neck, playing a different shape on each beat in three-string sweeps. After that, in bar 4, I play an Esus4 arpeggio on beats 1 and 2 and then resolve that back to the E major triad. *Sus4* means you just replace the 3rd of the chord/arpeggio with the diatonic 4th.

After the first four bars repeat, I move the sus4 to a major arpeggio sequence down the neck in whole steps, changing key every two bars. That sequence finally concludes on Asus4 (where I change direction, now starting on the 3rd string ) to A major, ending with a descending five-string sweep. The move to A major sets up the modulation (key change) to D minor/harmonic minor. The D minor arpeggios move up the neck in a combination of three- and five-string inversions. Since they're all the same note value, they work well together and flow quite nicely.

Then, on to G minor—the diatonic IV minor chord in the key. Once again that ascending multiple inversion three-string/five-string combination is applied.

You'll also notice that in three of the four bars of the G minor section, I'm using that previously covered five-string figure-8 pattern: descending one five-string shape and linking it to become the next one. On all of these G minor figure 8's, I'm always playing the tonic G (10th fret, 5th string) with my 1st finger. The previous D minor section then repeats and is followed up with a four-string, two-octave D harmonic minor run. I use economy picking on this run approaching each string on a down stroke, picking three notes per string down/up/down. The D minor section then resolves on an alternate picked harmonic minor neo-classical scale fragment.

The final six bars might be the most challenging, but once again, you'll notice I'm playing arpeggio shapes and sweeping patterns that we've previously covered, so that should certainly make things easier. In the first three bars of these final six, the pattern remains consistent: that five-note/quintuplet three-string diminished 7 arpeggio (C#°7) moving to an ascending-only five-string D minor sweep. I really like the aggressive sound that ascending-only sweeping gives you.

The piece finally ends with a fast three-string combination of D minor, A major, and then C# diminished 7, resolving to a five-string D minor shape. You can see that changing shapes on each beat can be challenging (especially at rapid speeds), and this piece remains one of my more demanding arpeggio excerpts.

# Prelude

54, 55

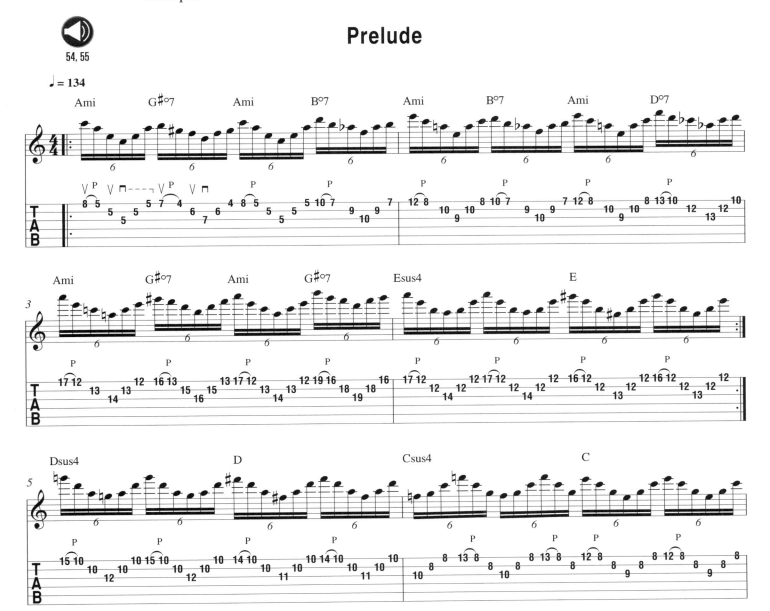

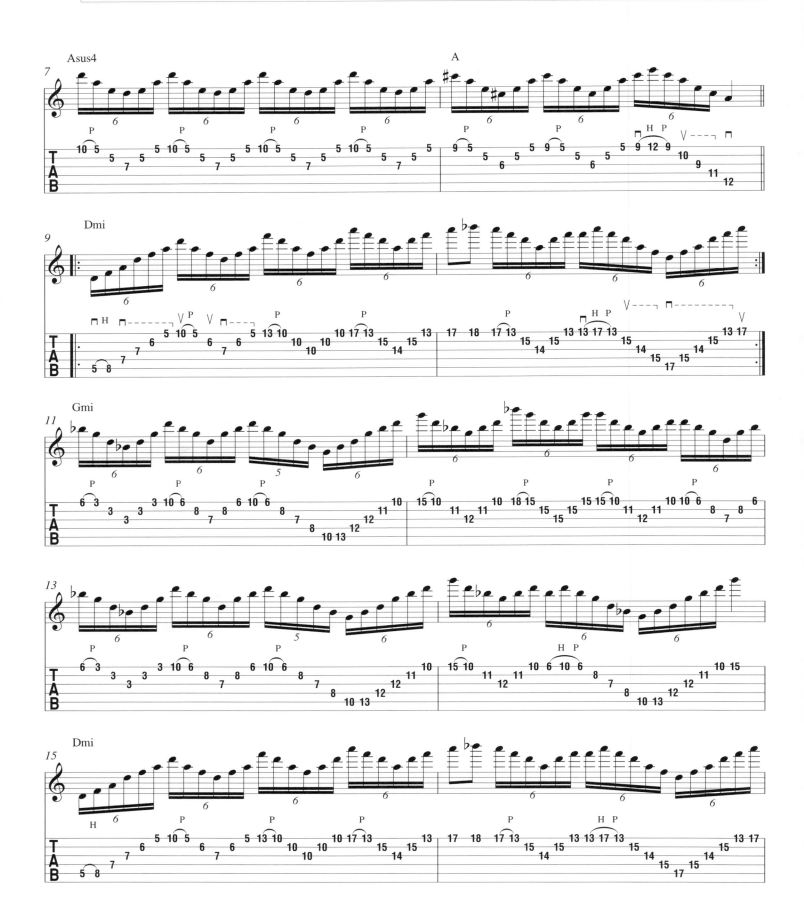

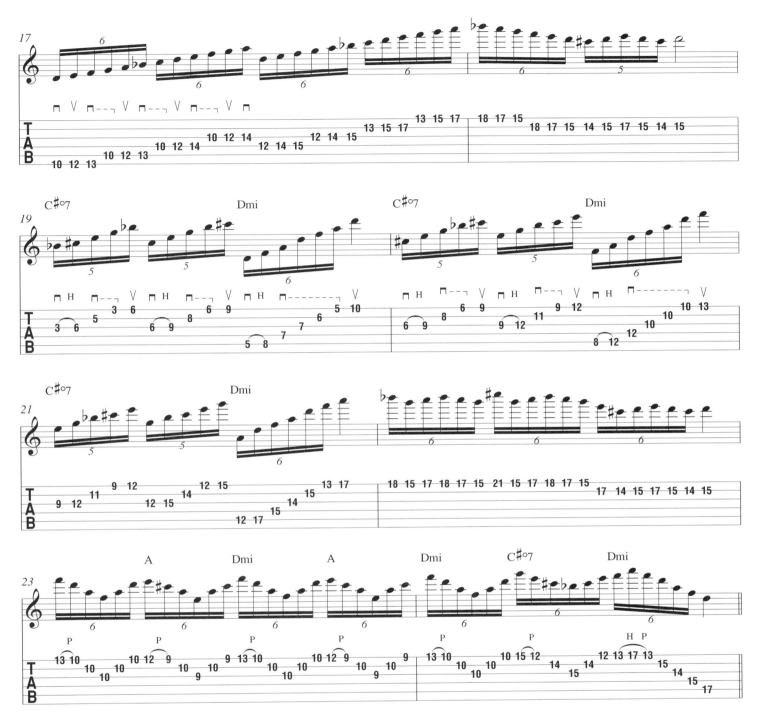

**FIG. 6.1.** "Prelude"

## "DEMON'S EYE"

The tune is from my 1996 release *Supersonic Shred Machine* and remains one of my more popular tracks, to this day. At this point, you should know the drill, so there's not a ton for me to say on this one, regarding new techniques.

In the key of D natural/harmonic minor, the tempo is quite fast (quarter note=130), and like "Prelude," in the first eight bars, you're continuously moving to a different inversion on each beat. That in itself is fairly demanding, but the toughest part is the one five-string arpeggio at the end of each of the first four bars. It's one thing blazing up consecutive five-string sweeps, but when you're playing all three-string shapes and then all of a sudden have to execute a five-string in the midst of those, it's far more difficult.

The second half of the arpeggio excerpt continues in the key moving to the relative major F and playing each arpeggio twice (F, C, B♭, to D minor, then A major back to D minor). Like the first eight bars, the endings have that identical three-string/five-string cadence. I'm still quite fond of this arpeggio section and really like the strong classical influence it has.

## Demon's Eye
### Arpeggio Section

56, 57

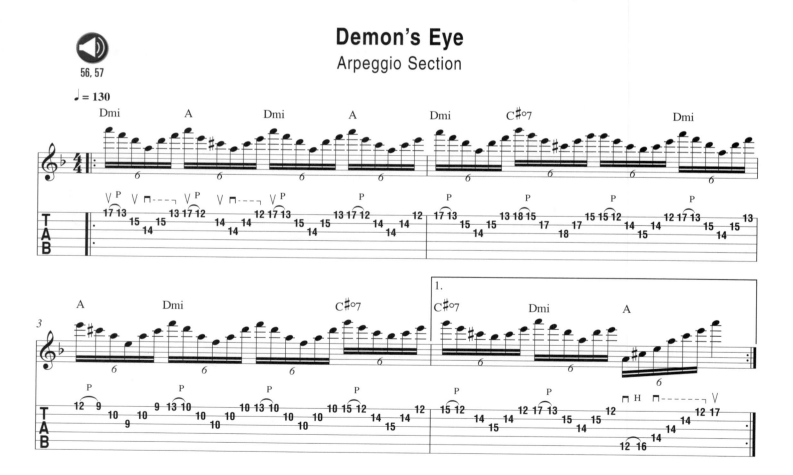

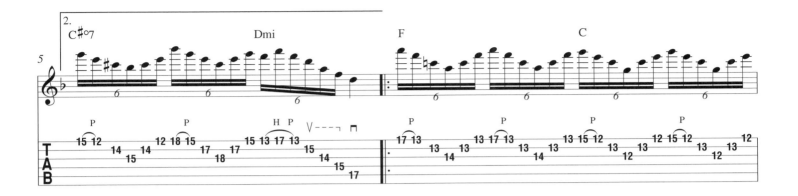

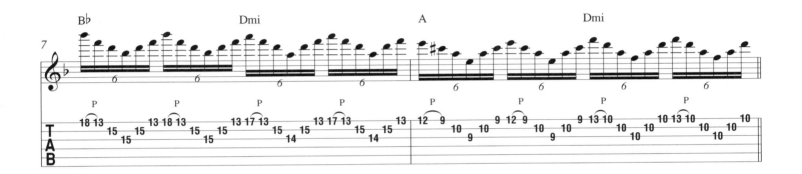

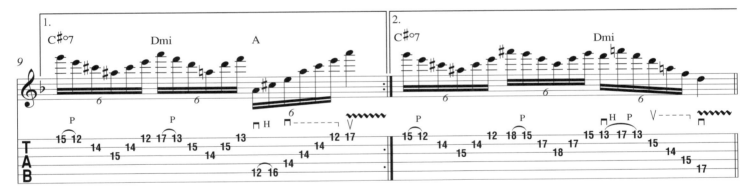

**FIG. 6.2.** "Demon's Eye"

## "THE DARK LORD'S ALLEGRO"

From my latest solo record, *The Dark Lord Rises*, this excerpt contains a really nice melodic combination of two-, three-, and five-string sweep shapes. The chord sequence repeats employing a composing technique I use quite frequently. The first time through, I play smaller two/three shapes and then build the arpeggio section up the second time making it more intense and complex with the larger more complex arpeggio patterns/shapes.

The chord sequence itself is in the combination B Aeolian/B harmonic minor, and I'm using a two-string, sixteenth-note sweeping pattern for pretty much the entire first time through (with the exception of the three-string E minor/F♯ major bar). This two-string pattern was covered way back in chapter 1. The second time through, I combine three- and five-string sweeps and then finish up by adding a six-string shape in the final bar.

All of these inversions and multi-string sweep combinations have been covered in previous chapters, but seeing them all intertwined in context really illustrates the many options available when you're trying to compose your own arpeggio sections/solo ideas.

# The Dark Lord's Allegro
## Arpeggio Section

58, 59

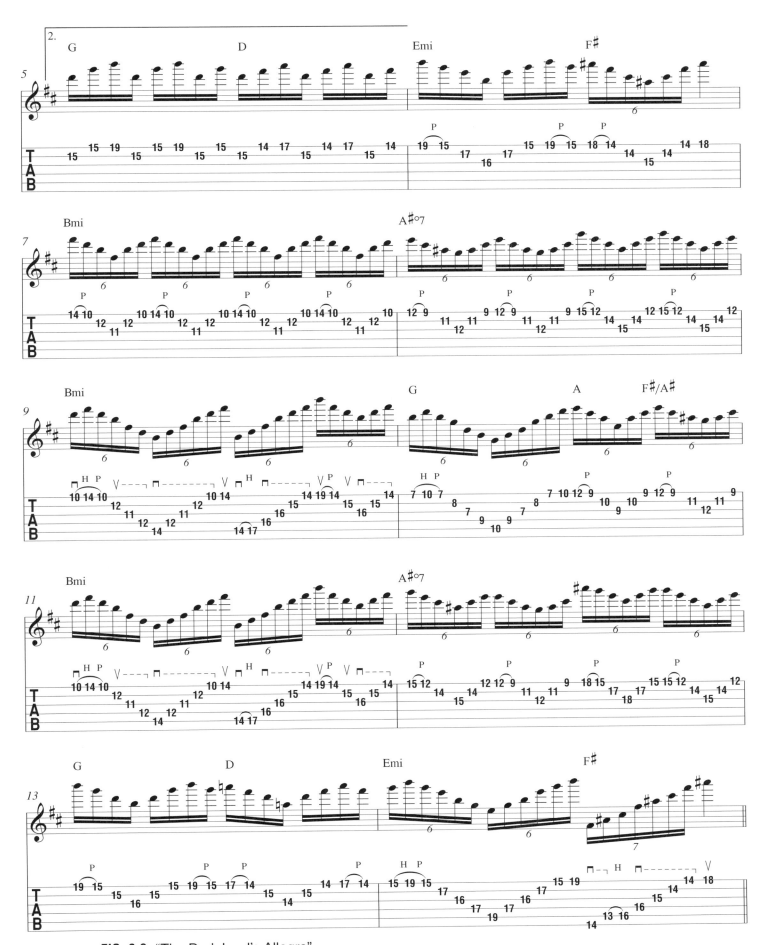

**FIG. 6.3.** "The Dark Lord's Allegro"

# Advanced Arpeggio Play

In chapter 7, I'll be introducing some larger sweep shapes as well as some technically demanding and more intense arpeggio combinations.

It's now time to up the ante, technique-wise, with some bigger, more extreme sweeps. This first one is a full six-string major shape, based off the root six-string E major barre chord at the 12th fret. I play this one with the third of the chord on the 5th string but you could move it to the 6th string (sixteenth fret) if that works better for you. The picking pattern is notated in figure 7.1, and as you can see, it is consistent with everything we've covered thus far.

I start on consecutive downs and then hammer-on the second note on the 5th string (pulling it off when I'm descending). The most difficult part about this (as well as some other examples in this chapter) is where I'm playing seven notes per beat. As I've stated previously, odd groupings are tough in that the slower you play them, the more awkward they are. The seven-note grouping (or "septuplet") is one of the hardest. If you compare this to an even sixteenth-note triplet/six-note grouping, you can see that just adding one extra note drastically changes the degree of difficulty.

60

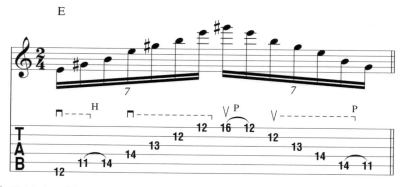

**FIG. 7.1.** E Major Shape 1

Figure 7.2 has the same E major shape as figure 7.1, except this time, I left the 3rd of the arpeggio (G♯) out in the lower octave. By doing this, it now becomes easier to handle: an even sixteenth-note sextuplet. This gives you the effect of the larger six-string sweep without having to deal with that seven-note grouping, I'm also combining it with a three-string sweep in the second half of the example (something I do quite frequently with six-string shapes).

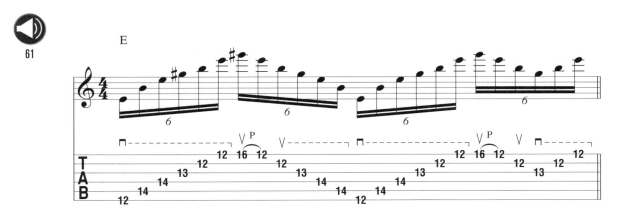

**FIG. 7.2.** E Major Shape 2

Figure 7.3 is a full six-string B minor sweep. I'm using the easiest inversion of the minor triad for my fretting hand. If you want to make an arpeggio shape larger, you can just keep stacking the chord tones to it, adding additional strings. Once again, it's a seven-note grouping, so this one will require some work to execute properly.

Note: While you can take any previously covered five-string arpeggio inversion and turn it into a six-string sweep, in this chapter, I'm focusing on the ones I use the most.

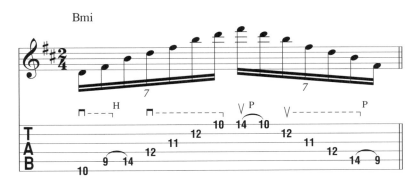

**FIG. 7.3.** B Minor Sweep 1

Another full six-string B minor shape combined with a three-string sweep, the example in figure 7.4 clearly outlines the B minor barre chord with the root on the 7th fret. This one combines a seven-note grouping on beat 1 with a standard sextuplet on beat 2. Most players find this fret-hand inversion shape by far the most difficult due to amount of barring it requires.

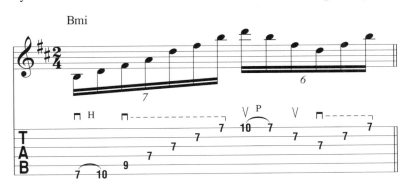

**FIG. 7.4.** B Minor Sweep 2

Figure 7.5 introduces the *tap-and-sweep* technique, once again on a B minor triad. I tap the root of the arpeggio on the 19th fret and then use pull-offs on the next two chord tones. I then move my pick-hand back to its standard position and execute the rest of the sweep in the standard five-string manner (as usual, the picking is notated). In measure 2, I'm tapping a small three-string shape. I once again tap the root and pull-off the next two tones (as I did previously). Then, using my fret hand, I hammer-on the other two remaining notes on the 2nd and 3rd string. So, there is no pick-hand action whatsoever on the first two beats of the measure. In the second half of the measure, the larger shape from the measure just repeats.

**FIG. 7.5.** B Minor Tap and Sweep

Figure 7.6 shows an A major tap-and-sweep lick. This is a prime example of how an arpeggio lick can become more intense sounding by just combining a few different patterns that, when played on their own, would sound fairly standard and somewhat pedestrian.

Here, I'm using the open C shape inversion, starting with that sextuplet five-string pattern I'm so fond of, with the hammer-on and pull-off. I then play the tap-and-sweep pattern from the last example. In bar 2, I play a five-string/three-string combination and then return to the tap-and-sweep pattern. You can see how the tap-and-sweep lick takes on a much greater intensity when combined with other sweeping patterns.

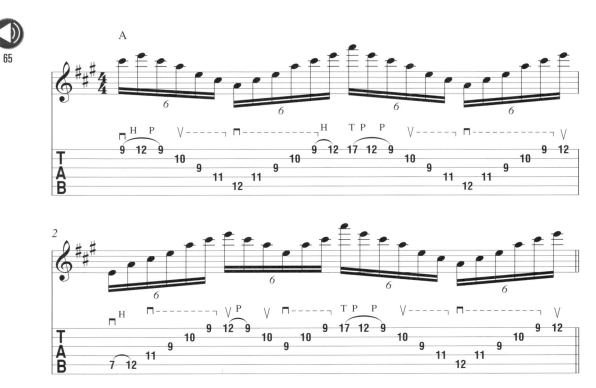

**FIG. 7.6.** A Major Tap and Sweep

The example in figure 7.7 is fairly extreme and a bit more technically demanding. I'm taking that six-string E major shape from the first example, and now I'm playing it only ascending. I love the aggressive/in-your-face sound that this produces, and when played at rapid speeds, it's pretty scary. This lick is something I'd play in an E Phrygian dominant (the fifth mode of A harmonic minor) groove. The first time, I stop on the ♭7 D (15th fret, 2nd string, technically making it an E dominant 7 arpeggio); the second time through, I play two notes on the top string. Rhythmically, it's no picnic, with the seven- and then eight-note groupings played consecutively. After that, I once again move to my go-to five-string lick and finish up with another seven-note six-string sweep outlining the root-5 E major barre chord at the 7th fret.

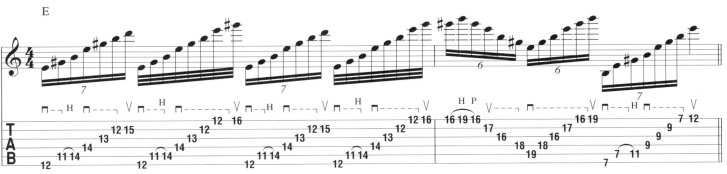

**FIG. 7.7.** E Major Shape Ascending

## "STRAT OUTA HELL"

This is a solo guitar track from my 2012 release *Revenge of the Shredlord*. This classically inspired arpeggio section is without a doubt the most technically demanding piece thus far. It was inspired by the great violin works of Antonio Vivaldi and Nicolo Paganini, as well as Swedish guitar legend Yngwie Malmsteen (all three, big influences of mine). The piece combines combinations of two-through six-string arpeggios played in various shapes and inversions.

### Strat Outa Hell
Revenge of the Shredlord

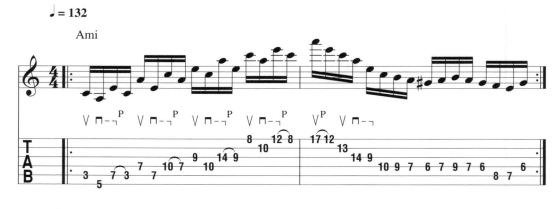

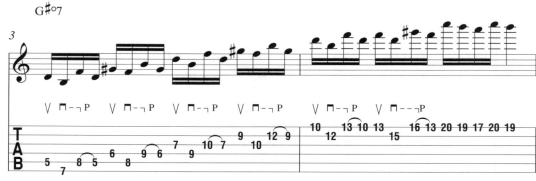

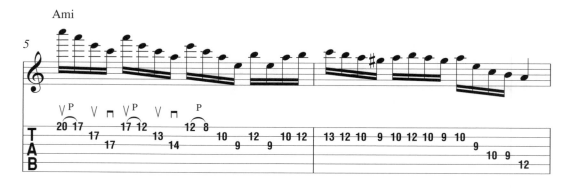

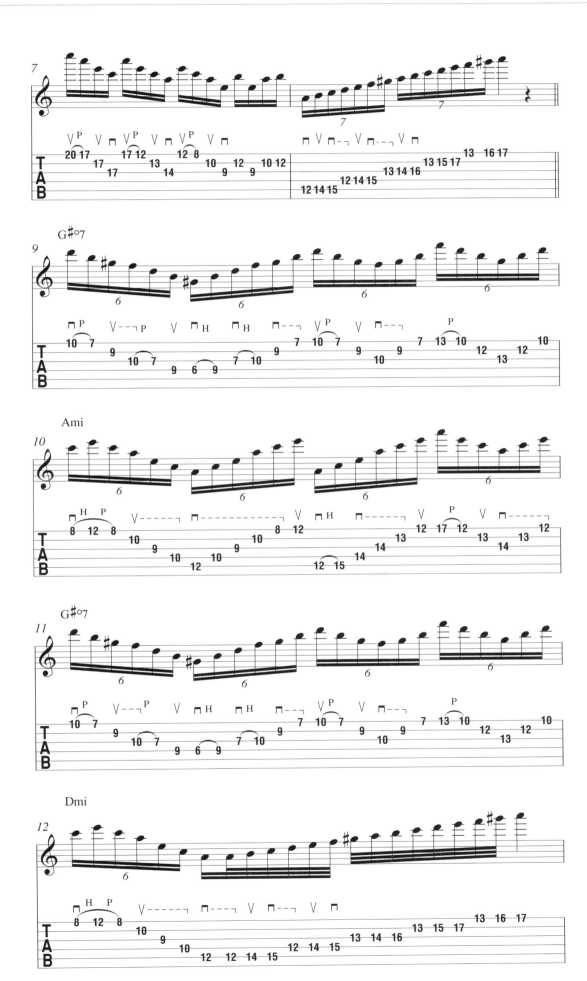

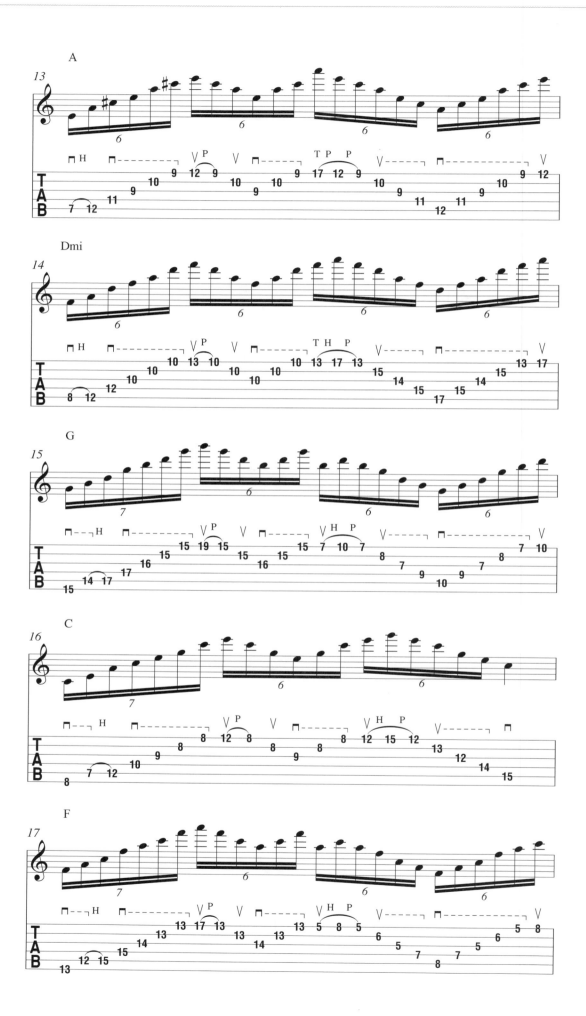

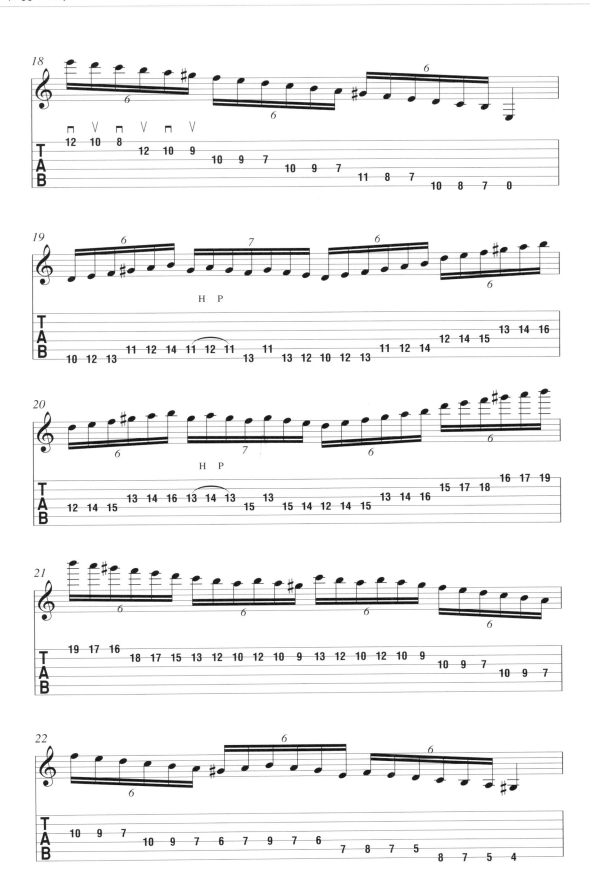

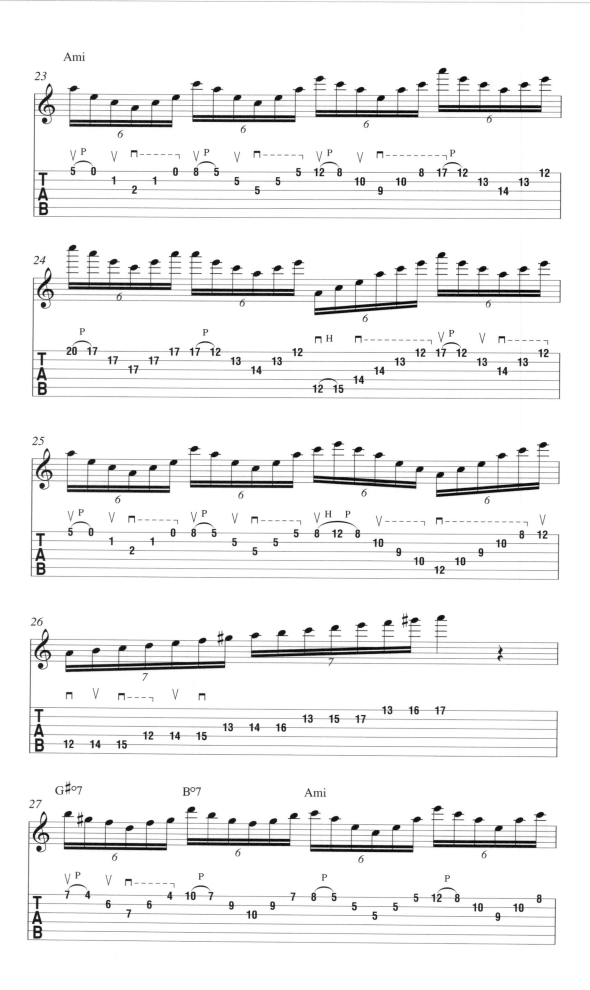

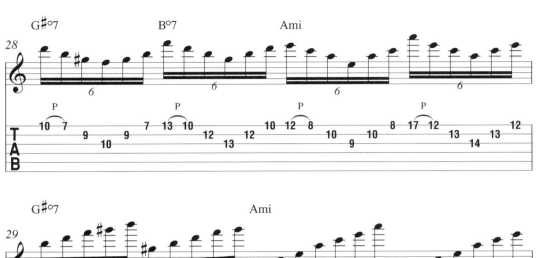

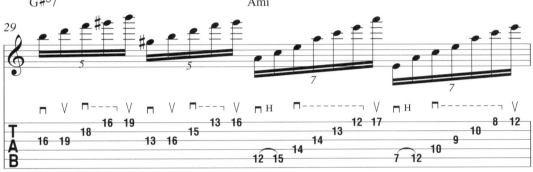

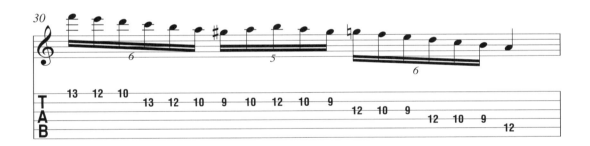

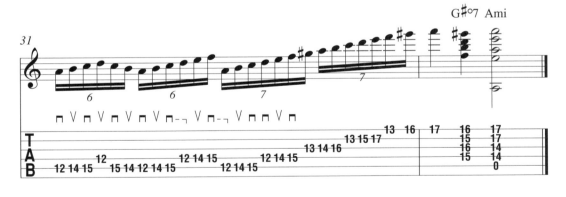

**FIG. 7.8.** "Strat Outa Hell"

"Strat Outa Hell" starts with an A minor arpeggio, using a violin arpeggio technique where I'm playing a higher chord tone and then going back to the next lower note in the arpeggio. Instead of playing it across the strings in position, in a block triadic shape, I'm breaking the multi-octave arpeggio up into smaller two-string shapes, moving up the neck (starting with an up stroke). The second measure ends with another violin type of idea where I play the A minor arpeggio and add the second degree of the scale, finishing with a harmonic minor classically influenced line. After the first two bars are repeated, I go to G♯ diminished 7 and apply that same classical technique from measure 1 where I play the higher note in the arpeggio going back to the next lower chord tone. In the diminished arpeggio, this flows a bit easier, as I'm just using that diagonal/symetrical type of fingering for the diminished 7 shape moving up and across the strings. Then, to finish this first section of the piece, it's back to A minor played in three-string sweeps but in a descending sixteenth-note rhythm where I pick them starting with an up stroke, then a pull-off, then another up stroke, followed by a down. After the three-string sweeps, it's a harmonic minor line followed by an arpeggio I use quite a bit where I add the second scale tone along with the leading tone (7th degree of the harmonic minor scale) to the triad. The section finishes up with an economy-picked ascending scale run in A harmonic minor.

The next section of the piece begins with the full four-string diminished 7 arpeggio (using hammer-ons and pull-offs when there are two notes on a string), going to a standard three-string diminished sweep, moving to A minor five-string inversions. The second time around, I once again add an ascending scale run—a very cool way to connect the run to that descending five-string A minor shape.

Following the diminished-to-minor section, I now go to a Bach inspired harmonic sequence A major- five-string/three-string combination, then tap and sweep to a D minor five-string combination. (Note: All of these shapes and sweep patterns should be fairly familiar to you by now, as we've covered them previously.)

On the next set of bars with G, C, and F major, I play the same lick on each, playing a six-string/three-string combination then linking that to the easy-to-play five-string open C shape. And yes, once again, it's that five-string sextuplet lick with the hammer-on and pull-off I'm so fond of. Yeah, I'm playing that any chance I get. Why? Beause it's easy and sounds cool.

After the major arpeggios it's a descending alternate-picked single-note harmonic minor/dominant Phrygian scale line. In the next four measures (mm. 19–22), it's a combination of alternate- and economy-picked single-note shred in Phrygian dominant. In measure 19, I start off with a very cool three-octave hexatonic (six note) diminished shape where I just add the additional scale tone from harmonic minor to the diminished 7 arpeggio (which works great in Phrygian dominant).

In the final section, it's back to arpeggios: three-string A minor inversions moving up the neck (yeah, that Yngwie-inspired open-position one takes some getting used to) and combined with a few five-string shapes. After the A harmonic minor ascending run, I alternate between G♯ diminished 7 and A minor in three-string inversions moving up the neck. Changing inversions on each beat can be challenging.

The last arpeggio lick in the piece (m. 29) might be my favorite. I use that ascending-only technique I favor, where I play two diminished 7 quintuplet (five-note) arpeggios followed by two seven-note/ascending-only five-string A minor sweeps.

The piece ends with a descending mixed minor run (violin/Yngwie Malmsteen/Uli Jon Roth inspired scale shape, where you include the 7th degrees of both natural and harmonic minor). Last is a combined alternate-/economy-picked ascending harmonic-minor scale run. Like I said, this one's quite technically demanding. There's quite a bit of very useful info between all of the violin-inspired arpeggio play and classically influenced single-note linear action.

## "THE WITCHING HOUR"

This excerpt from "The Witching Hour" is another one of my more extreme/technically difficult arpeggio sections. This track is from my 2009 release *Virtuosic Vendetta* and was heavily inspired by the Yngwie Malmsteen classic "Black Star." Like "Strat Outa Hell," it combines many sweeping string combinations along with classically influenced single-note lines.

68, 69

## The Witching Hour

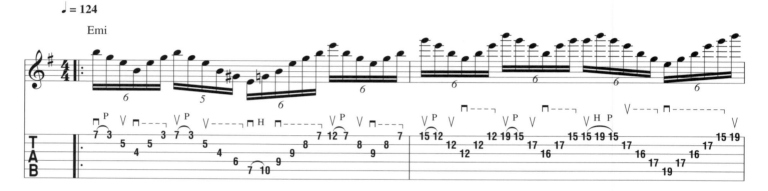

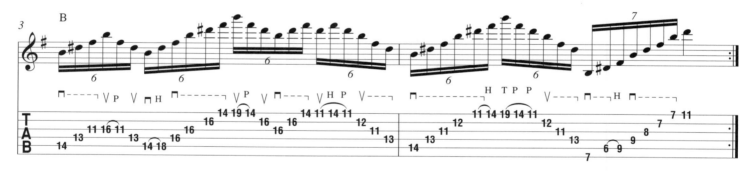

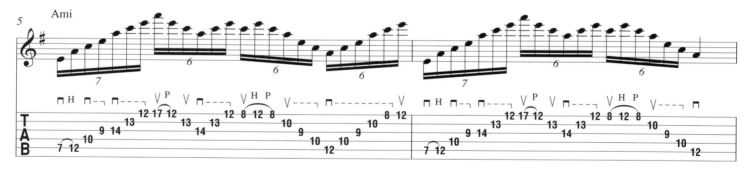

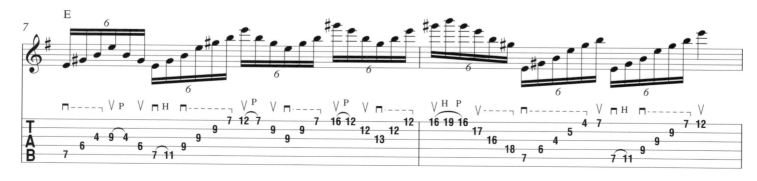

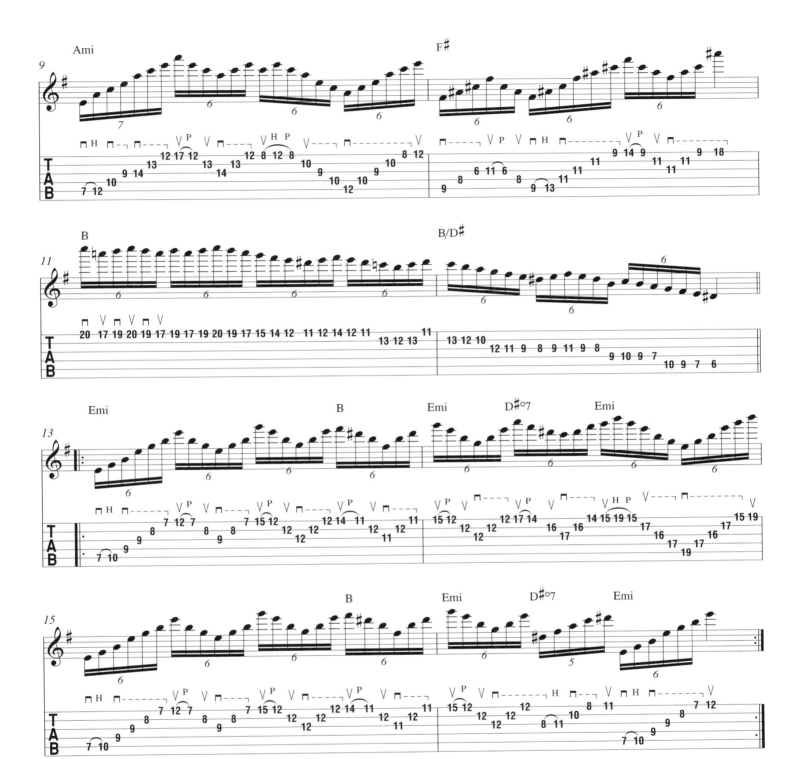

**FIG. 7.9.** "The Witching Hour"

"The Witching Hour" is in the key of E natural/harmonic minor and begins with a three-string/five-string combination of E minor triadic inversions moving up the neck. (Note: On beats 2 and 3 of measure 1, I'm connecting those two E minor five-string inversions with that figure-eight pattern discussed earlier, using my first finger at the 7th fret, 5th string). After that, I go to B major and play a fairly intense sweep combination. It starts with a three-string B major sweep starting on the 5th string. While three-string sweeps are most commonly used and played on the top three strings, you can find those inversions on multiple string sets. I then link that to a root position five-string/three-string combination that starts at the 14th fret. In the following measure, it's that tap-and-sweep major arpeggio pattern discussed at the beginning of this chapter, followed by an ascending-only full six-string B major sweep. To work up these intense two measures of B major, first, make sure you are able to execute all of the shapes/patterns individually before trying to combine them consecutively.

After the first four measures repeat, it goes to A minor (the IV minor chord in E minor). The first A minor shape (first two beats of the measure) is a bit unusual in that I combine two different inversion shapes connecting them on the 3rd string. It might seem strange to play consecutive down strokes on the 3rd string, but it works fine for me, since I'm shifting position.

Once again, you have that tricky seven-note grouping to start the A minor section. I link that to that standard five-string (open D minor inversion) A minor shape. The second measure of A minor is identical except I descend only on the last portion of measure. Following the A minor, it goes to E major for two bars. It's first a three-string sweep on strings 5, 4, and 3, followed by a five-string/three-string combination. The first measure of E major ends with a three-string sweep on beat 4.

The next measure opens with that easy six-note open C shape, but this time, with an octave jump on the ascending end of it. (The octave jump ups the degree of difficulty, plus it looks cool when you play it.) The measure ends with a root position five-string ascending sweep finishing on the root.

The two measures of E once again illustrate how intense these simple triadic shapes can get when you combine and connect them.

We're then back to A minor. The previously played shapes are just repeated. This time, following A minor, I go to F♯ major (secondary dominant making a V I resolution to the B major which is the V chord in E harmonic minor).

The first three beats of the F♯ major are identical to the E major section, just played two frets higher. I slide all the way up to the 3rd of the triad A♯ (18th fret) on beat 4 of the measure, to finish out. Then two measures of fast alternate-picked lines in B Phrygian dominant resolve to E minor.

The next four measures mix E minor, B major, and D♯ diminished 7 in five- and three-string combinations. By this time, all of these inversions, patterns, and combinations should be quite easy to recognize. This section of "The Witching Hour" finishes up with multi-octave, descending, single-note lines in E minor and concludes with a three-note-per-string economy-picked ascending harmonic minor run.

In both "The Witching Hour" and "Strat Outa Hell," I combine sweep-picking arpeggio play with economy- and alternate-picked lines. You can see that executing each one of these techniques individually is one thing, but combining, connecting, and controlling them is a whole other story.

## "BULLET TRAIN"

"Bullet Train" appears on an older release of mine, *A Shred Odyssey* (2001), but the better known version is from the green screen YouTube video "Joe Stump in the Studio," where I'm playing it live with a backing track during a DVD shoot. Figure 7.10 presents the introduction.

The first three bars are all played legato; I tap the root note of each arpeggio, pull-off the remaining notes on the top string, and then hammer-on the rest of the arpeggio with my fret-hand on strings 2 and 3. And yes, they're all identical; the only thing changing is the arpeggio shape: Am to G to F. In the fourth measure, I go to an E major five-string tap-and-sweep hammering on the descending portion of the shape and down-sweeping the ascending part.

After the E major, on beats 3 and 4 it goes F major to G, and those tapped/legato three-string shapes repeat. The chord sequence then starts over, this time with all five-string tap-and-sweep shapes. The A minor, G major, and F major arpeggios are all played identically to the way I played the larger E major shape at the start of the fourth measure: tapping the root, pulling off then hammering on strings 2, 3, and 4 on the way down, then sweeping the ascending portion of each arpeggio with all down strokes.

The intro concludes with an ascending three-string G♯ diminished 7 arpeggio climb, moving up in minor thirds (three frets at a time).

# Bullet Train Intro

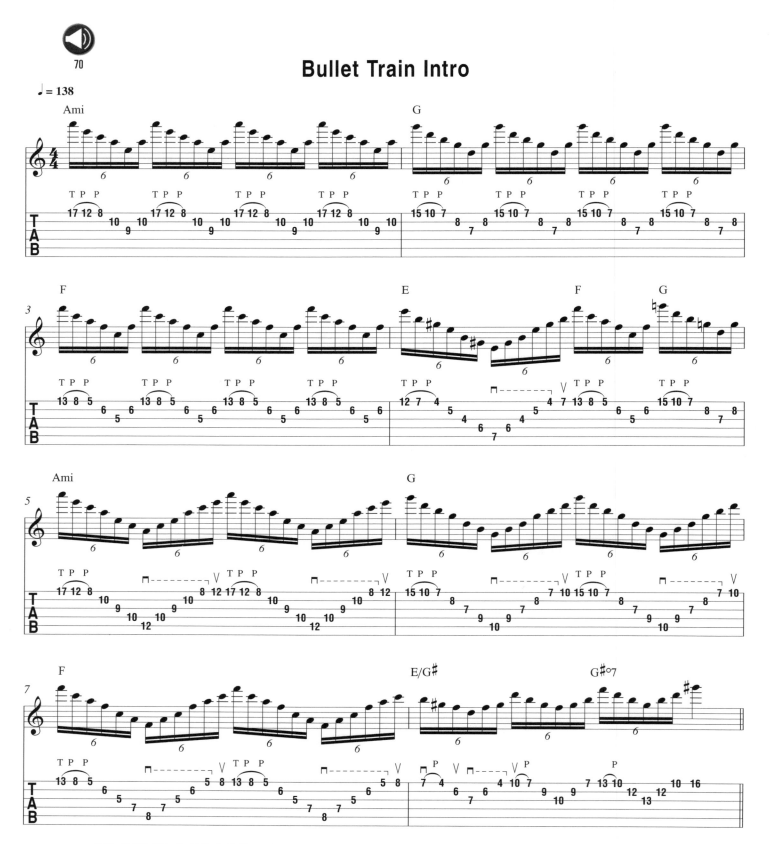

FIG. 7.10. "Bullet Train" (Intro)

**CHAPTER 8**

# Broken Arpeggios/Classically Influenced Sequences

In chapter 8, I'll be breaking down two arpeggio sections of mine. Both of these are very classically influenced, as well as primarily triplet-based. I'm using what I refer to as *broken/sequencial arpeggio patterns* in both.

Just as you can play a scale in a diatonic/numerical sequence (e.g., moving up/down the scale three or four notes at time), you can do the same with an arpeggio. This type of sequencing stems back from the great classical composers (Bach, Vivaldi, Handel, Mozart, Beethoven). As early as the late 1970s and early '80s, what I refer to as the "Holy Trinity of European hard rock/metal guitar," Ritchie Blackmore, Uli Jon Roth, and Michael Schenker (and later Yngwie Malmsteen, of course) adapted these ideas and started using them in a hard rock and metal context.

## "RBNCSF NO. II"

"RBNCSF No. II" is from my 1996 release *Super Sonic Shred Machine*. The acronym stands for "Ritchie Blackmore's Neo-Classical Shredfest Number Two," as the main melody is taken from the small arpeggio bit Blackmore does towards the end of the solo in Deep Purple's "Child in Time." The chord progression in the first sixteen bars is that classic one I borrowed from J.S. Bach (Ami Dmi G C F B♭ E B°7 G♯°) and have used quite a few times.

I start out by playing the arpeggios in groups of three's, meaning, I start on the root of the A minor, move up three notes in the arpeggio, then go to the next higher chord tone (the 3), and once again move up three notes. This three-note numerical pattern continues throughout the measure. The picking pattern I use is notated in measure 1; I'm going down/down/up. While picking it this way is a combination of alternate and sweep/economy picking, the pattern sounds more alternate picked than it does swept.

In the following measure, over the D minor, I play the same exact three-note pattern, just in the opposite direction descending and moving down the arpeggio three notes at a time. I pick this descending pattern down/up/down starting on another down stroke every three notes. You can take my pick-hand suggestions on these, or you could try straight alternate picking, if you feel that works better for you. This three-note sequence continues on the next several measures over the G, C, and F major chords. Then on the B♭ major, I add a three-string sweep for variation. After the B♭, it's a five-string/three-string combination over the E chord moving to a three-string diminished 7 arpeggio. The chord progression then repeats for the next eight bars. For the first six bars, the arpeggio patterns remain consistent, where I play an ascending five-string/three-string combo on the first chord (Ami, G, F) and a descending five-string sweep on the second chord in the progression (Dmi, C, B♭).

I've previously covered the sweeping patterns in these first eight bars quite a few times. However, one thing that's different now is that I'm playing them fast, as triplets, as opposed to blazing them up in sixteenth-note triplets. Executing the sweeps evenly and cleanly in this fast triplet-based rhythm definitely utilizes a different type of technical command and control for your pick hand and synchronization.

After the the B♭, it once again goes to E major. This time, I use a larger multi-octave shape. I start out with a small two-string arpeggio on the lower strings at the 12th fret, and link that to the standard (open C) E major shape at the 19th fret. I then return to a smaller two-string shape, this time on the top two strings and then employ an octave jump down to fourth position.

For the next six bars, I'm playing some single note (Uli-Jon Roth/Malmsteen inspired) neo-classical lines in harmonic minor/Phrygian dominant. In the first four bars, I play a short two-bar phrase in two octaves. In the last two bars, it's a one-bar phrase moving down the scale in seconds (i.e., you play a higher scale tone then move down to the next lowest scale tone). I play this one-measure seconds lick also in two octaves. You can see playing solo/melodic ideas in multiple octaves really helps you to stretch them further.

Following the two octave seconds lick is a diminished 7 arpeggio played in that two-string diagonal fingering in quarter-note triplets, moving to some two-string diads (i.e., two-note chords; F to E both with the root and 3 of the chord). Following the diads, it's more single-note action, playing up the A harmonic minor scale in a four-note sequence. I move up the scale four notes at a time in triplets, executing this pattern as I do many single-note passages: with a combination of alternate and economy picking.

In measures 29 to 31, I use an extremely cool classically influenced/neo-classical pattern where I'm playing what I call a "classical approach-tone arpeggio lick." The arpeggio is A minor, and I play a note a half step/one fret lower than each chord tone inside the arpeggio. I play this pattern in an ascending three-note sequence and use economy picking throughout picking down/up/down. To finish the piece, it's G♯ diminished 7 to A minor in multiple three-string inversions. Then I go to another triplet-based ascending four-note sequence. The final bar is a blazing economy-picked three-note-per-string run, straight up A harmonic minor.

## RBNCSF No. 2

Joe Stump

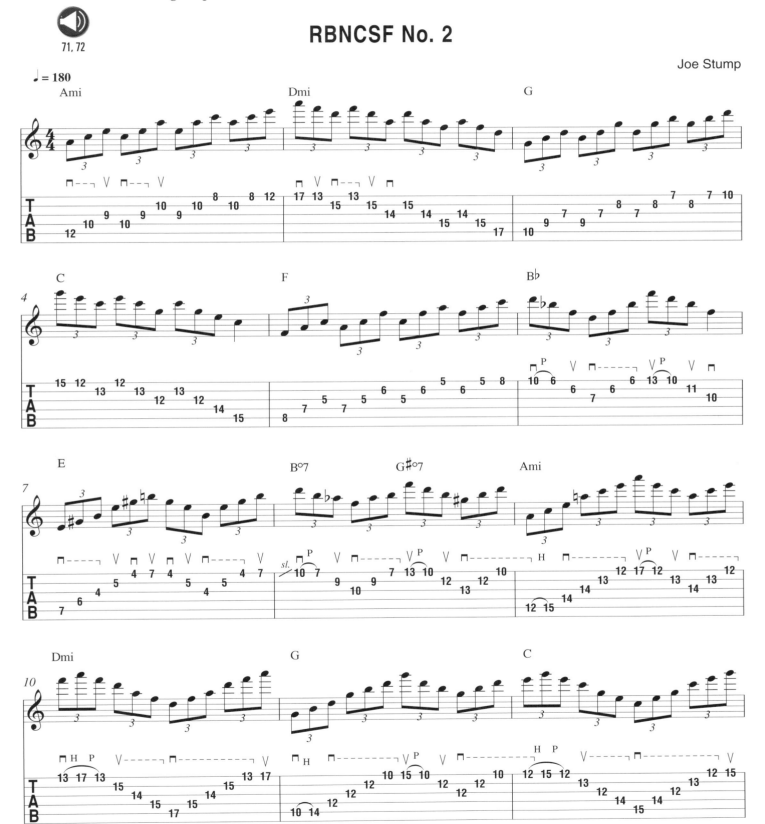

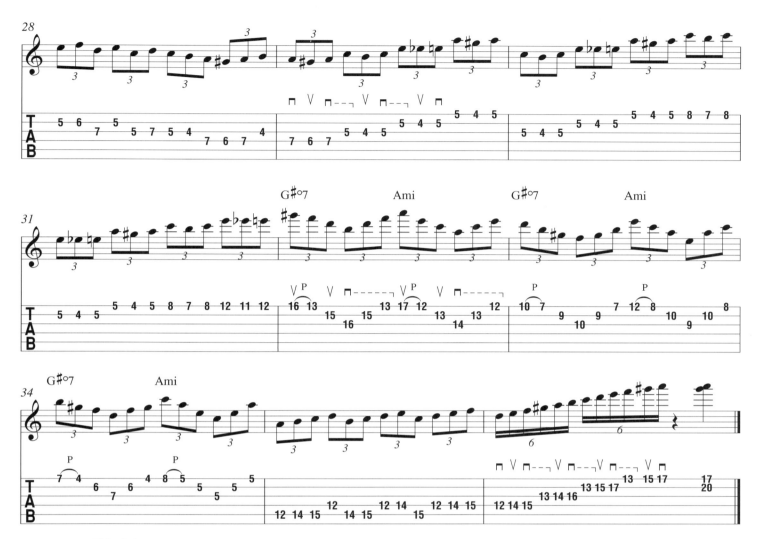

FIG. 8.1. "RBNCSF No. II"

# "NEO-CLASSICAL SHREDFEST NO. 4"

"Neo-Classical Shredfest No. 4" is from my latest solo album *The Dark Lord Rises*. As you can probably guess by the title, it's another technically demanding neo-classical arpeggio section. This one involves more classically influenced broken arpeggio play, as well as a host of other techniques. It's in the key of B minor/harmonic minor. Like " RBNCSF No. II," it is predominantly triplet-based.

It begins by moving down a B minor arpeggio in groups of three's (the same three-note pattern featured previously). After the descending three's, I play a five-string/three-string combination and then go to that tap-and-sweep technique, tapping the root of the B minor arpeggio at the 19th fret and then pulling off the 5th and 3rd of the triad with my fret hand. Following the tap-and-sweep in bar 3 in B minor, I descend down the standard five-string shape, but instead of sweeping, I alternate-pick when descending, sweeping down on the way back up.

In the next four bars, the sequencing is identical. The only thing that changes is the arpeggio shape from B minor to A♯ diminished 7 for two bars, and then to A♯ diminished triad for the tap-and-sweep/five-string portion. It then goes C to G to F♯ major, each two arpeggio bars apiece. (Note with the C major arpeggio, I'm once again using that flat II major chord derived from classical music.) The first bar of each major chord contains that broken arpeggio descending three-note pattern (picked the same way I did it in the first piece of this chapter: down/up/down) followed by a five-string/three-string combination.

The first sixteen bars conclude with three-string A♯ diminished 7 arpeggios with a triplet-based chromatic line added to each diminished shape. (I stole this lick from former Scorpions German guitar legend Uli-Jon Roth.) I execute the three-string diminished arpeggio with the standard sweep-picking pattern and then start back on a consecutive down stroke to play the chromatic line, alternate-picked.

The chord progression then repeats. This time, on the B minor, I use a different broken-arpeggio three-note pattern. I first encountered this arpeggio pattern playing some of Bach's violin sonatas and partitas, as well as some of his inventions. In this pattern, I play a lower note in the arpeggio and then go to the next highest in the shape and then return to the lower note. I cascade that pattern down the five-string B minor shape, keeping the three-note sequence constant throughout. After that, the same five-string/three-string sweep combination from bar 2 repeats.

In the final two bars of B minor, I start with root position five-string minor shape at the 14th fret. I play a three-string sweep on the top of the five-string, but this time, I play a line adding the leading tone/raised 7th from B harmonic minor to the small three-string arpeggio. I love this lick. It sounds extremely dark and classical. Combining lines with arpeggio shapes really makes things more interesting, musically.

After the B minor triadic lick with the leading tone, there's some Malmsteen-inspired single-note lines in harmonic minor. Some snakey harmonic minor phrasing ideas are followed by a blazing descending-scale run, played in a combination of across the strings and down the neck. The harmonic-minor single-note lines take the place of where the A♯ diminished 7 and triad arpeggios were, the first time through the chord sequence.

After that, it's back to C major, repeating the same information from the very first time through the progression. In the following two bars, over the G major, I use that same cascading three-note broken-arpeggio pattern (lower chord tone then to the next higher note) that I played over the B minor the second time through. This time, instead of playing it straight across a five-string shape, I move it down the neck on a single string using hammer-ons and pull-offs and link that to the five-string G major shape in 7th position. As per usual, all of the picking patterns are notated.

"Neo-Classical Shredfest No. 4" concludes with a five-string/three-string combination over F♯ major. Then once again, I go to that diminished/chromatic Uli lick from the first time through, this time extending the chromatic lick, moving it up the neck a minor third (three frets).

Both of these pieces are quite challenging and technically demanding but in a completely different way than all of the things previously featured. This type of up-tempo triplet-based arpeggio/linear play will certainly add a new dimension of articulation, command, and control to your technique.

# Neo-Classical Shredfest No.4

Joe Stump

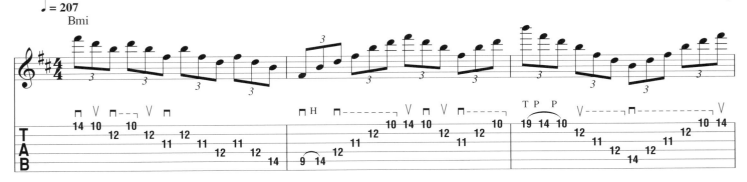

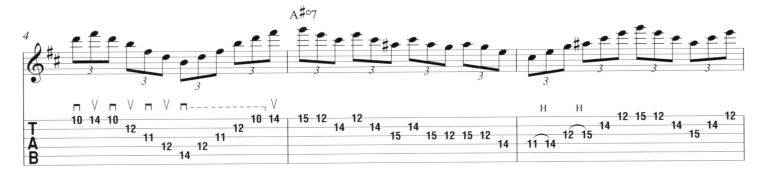

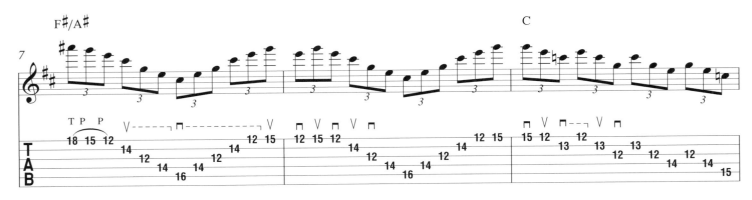

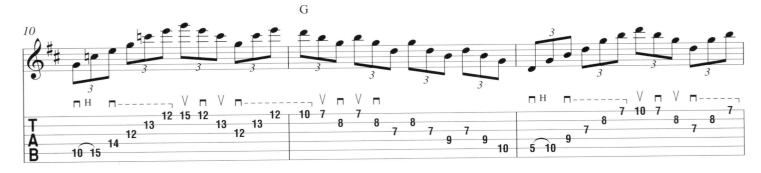

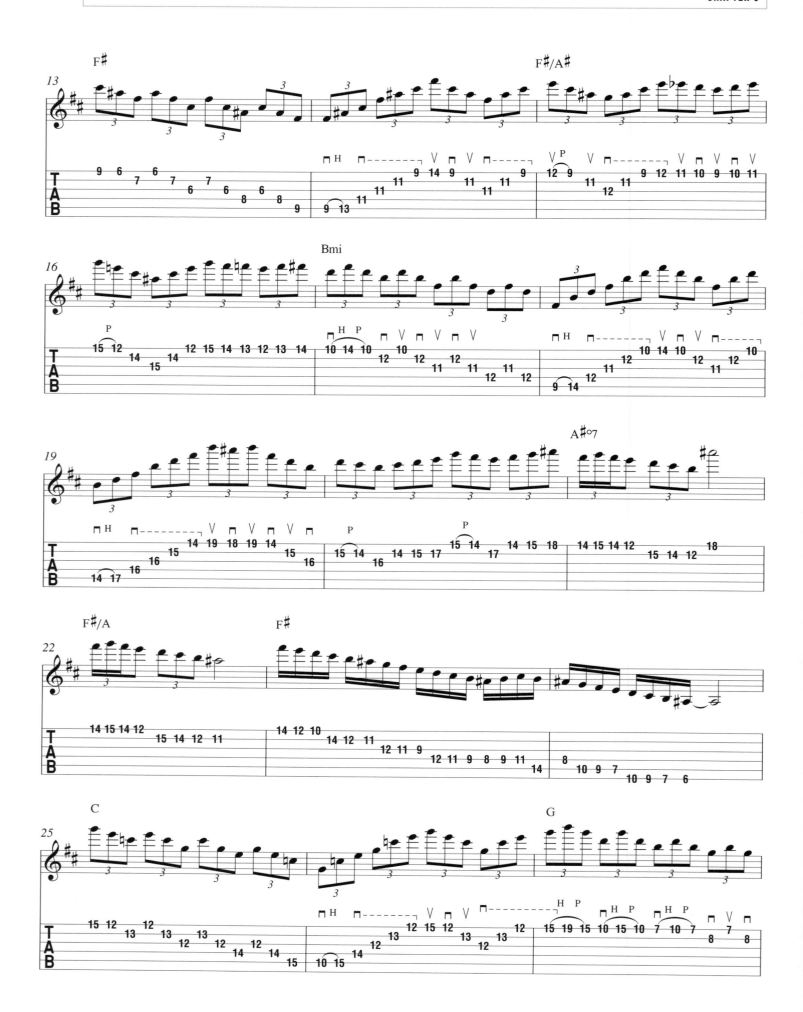

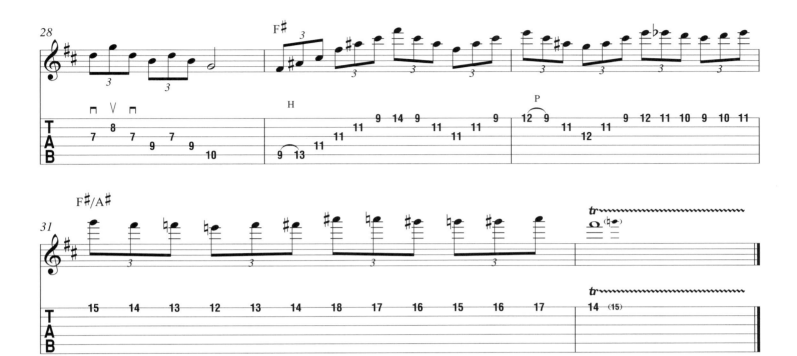

**FIG. 8.2.** "Neo-Classical Shredfest No. 4"

# String-Skipping Arpeggios

In chapter 9, I'll cover some string-skipping arpeggio shapes I like to use. I often mix them into scripted arpeggio sections, as they provide a nice contrast to sweep shapes.

Figure 9.1 is a string-skipping diminished-triad arpeggio. Most metal players are familiar with diminished 7 because it's commonly used in hard rock and metal, it sounds dark/sinister, and also because it's symmetrical. The diminished triad is not nearly as familiar. This one's a B diminished triad. From the root, I start with two consecutive down strokes and then add a hammer-on approaching the high E on an up stroke.

With all the string-skipping arpeggios in this chapter, I've provided the way I pick them and also where I add hammer-ons and pull-offs. However, all of this is somewhat subjective. Try different ways of picking to see what works for you.

75

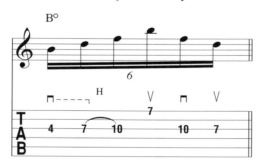

**FIG. 9.1.** String-Skipping B Diminished Triad Arpeggio

Figure 9.2 is another B diminished triad, this time in first inversion starting on the 3rd of the arpeggio. I start with an up stroke, add a pull-off on the top string, and then pick the rest of it. I'll also sometimes play this one more legato, depending on the tempo and sound I want. I'll also move these diminished triad shapes around symmetrically in minor thirds (three frets at a time) as I would a diminished 7 lick.

**FIG. 9.2.** First Inversion B Diminished Triad

Figure 9.3 is a C major string-skipping arpeggio. As you can see, I'm just taking a standard C major three-string sweep and moving the G to the 12th fret, 3rd string, as opposed to playing it on the 8th fret 2nd string (as I would in a three-string sweep shape). I'm also playing the arpeggio in a three-note sequence, moving down three chord tones at a time. The skip makes this pattern much easier to execute, as opposed to playing it inside a block sweep shape. My picking pattern's notated in figure 9.3, but you can try adding hammer-ons and pull-offs in different spots, as well as experimenting with varying pick strokes to see what works best for you.

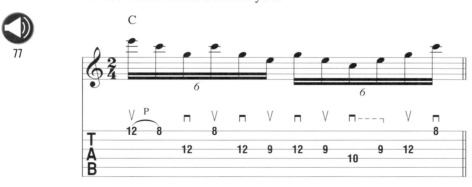

**FIG. 9.3.** C Major String-Skipping Arpeggio

Figure 9.4 is a D minor string skipping arpeggio in straight, even sixteenth notes. My first three examples were triplet/sextuplet-based, but like any type of lick or single-note idea, it's cool to vary the rhythm. This D minor first-inversion shape can also be quite tricky if you're playing it in a straight block three-string sweep, as it requires all that barring/rolling with the 1st finger of your fret hand. So once again, the string skip not only gives you a different open type sound, but it also makes executing the arpeggio in this particular pattern a bit easier.

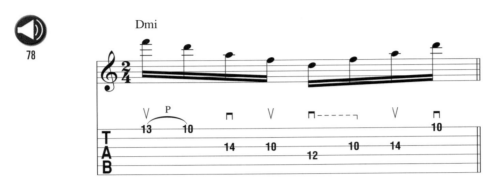

**FIG. 9.4.** D Minor String-Skipping Arpeggio

Figure 9.5 is a G♯ diminished 7 string-skipping arpeggio. I like to take a picking pattern/fragment I'd normally play on a set of strings inside a scale and plug it into this shape. If you are familiar with my music, it's no secret how fond I am of playing in harmonic/Hungarian minor and Phrygian strains of those scales, so I use this diminished shape quite frequently. The picking pattern is just a combination of a few different scale fragments.

The first beat is a single-string alternate-picked fragment. On beat 2, I'm employing a descending three's pattern. Beats 3 and 4 are back to two standard picking patterns. You might be familiar with these picking patterns, as they're somewhat common vocabulary for many metal players/shredders, but inside the diminished 7 shape, they're a bit tougher to identify. Aside from the one indicated pull-off in beat 2 (which you could just alternate-pick, but I think the pull-off sounds cool), I'm primarily alternate-picking this lick, with the exception of the string cross on the last part of beat 4, where I use economy picking. However that's just my take on it. It's far more common to alternate pick the entire example (with the exception of that one pull-off). As with all diminished 7 licks, I move this up in minor thirds. I'm using my 1st, 2nd, and 4th fingers throughout. Yeah, there's quite a bit of stretching involved, but it does look cool visually when you play it.

79

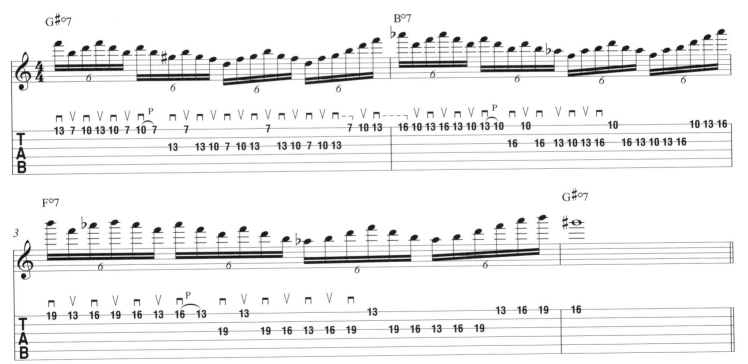

**FIG. 9.5.** G♯ Diminished 7 String-Skipping Arpeggio

Figure 9.6 is the intro "Man Your Battlestations," from my 2012 release *Revenge of the Shredlord*. I'm again using that dreaded string-skipping diminished lick. Also once again, I'm plugging a few different picking fragments into the shape. This one might seem a bit confusing, so I'll explain the varying picking patterns I'm using. On beats 1 and 2 of the first two measures, it's just a combination of two of the fragments from the previous example. Then on beat 3, I play a seconds-based descending scalar melodic pattern. I arrange the three different picking fragments (each a beat long) and just change the last beat in each measure of the two-bar phrase, ending on a different fragment each time.

I move the lick up symmetrically with a combination of alternate and economy picking, and then end with a blazing descending run in a combination of harmonic and mixed minor (i.e., the combination of natural and harmonic minor, containing the sevenths from both scales).

If you were to see or hear me play this lick, you might find it quite intimidating. But when I break it down and show you exactly how it works, by plugging in these commonly used picking fragments, it becomes a bit less scary.

80, 81

## Man Your Battlestations Intro

Joe Stump

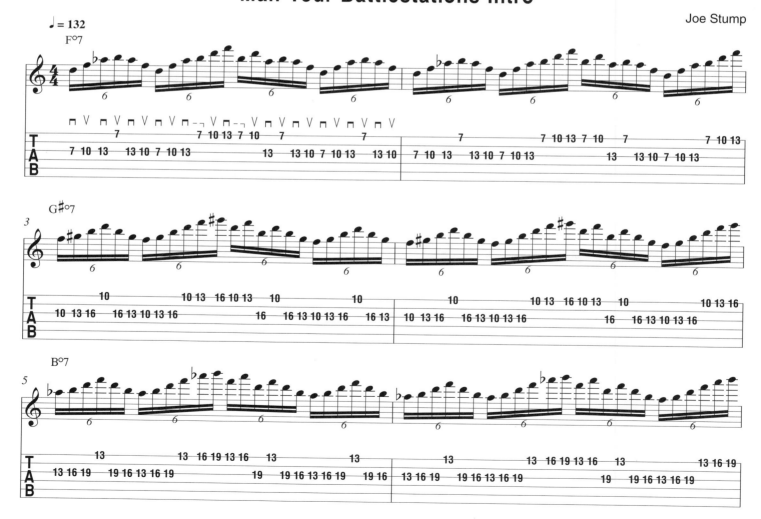

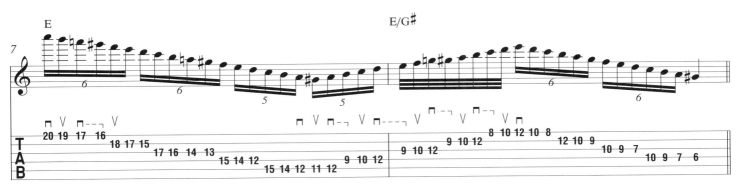

**FIG. 9.6.** "Man Your Battlestations" (Intro)

## "HOSTILE TAKEOVER"

This is the arpeggio section that follows the solo from the track "Hostile Takeover," from my 2015 release *The Dark Lord Rises*. It's a short, eight-bar arpeggio section containing a combination of string-skipping arpeggios and broken arpeggios as well as two-, three-, and six-string sweeps. In the first three bars, I'm playing that three-note descending sextuplet string-skipping pattern that was featured earlier in this chapter. (See figure 9.3 and note the picking pattern, but of course, it's also notated in the first measure of figure 9.7.) I just plug that lick into the chord sequence: A minor to B diminished to G# diminished.

Following the G# diminished triad arpeggio, I return to A minor, this time playing that broken arpeggio pattern across the A minor five-string shape descending three notes at a time (see chapter 8). I then complete measure 4 with a root position five-string sweep. In the next two bars, it's back to the string-skipping arpeggios (F to G). Note that on the actual recording, I'm playing sweep shapes on the F and G but included these string skips in the excerpt here for additional practice of this technique.

In bar 7, it goes back to G#, this time diminished 7 played in a descending two-string pattern using all down strokes and that one additional pull-off. (By now, you should be quite familiar with this two-string pattern, as it was featured in chapter 1.) The excerpt concludes with a vicious E major triad played in a combination of six- and three-string sweeps.

Once again, all of the picking patterns are notated, but other than the string skips, which are new in this chapter, all the other arpeggio info has been covered previously. Even though the section is short, it combines quite a few useful arpeggio techniques.

# Hostile Takeover
## String-Skipping Section (Intro)

Joe Stump

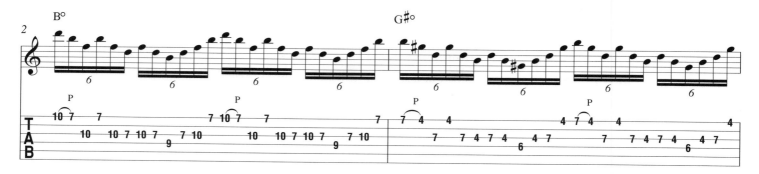

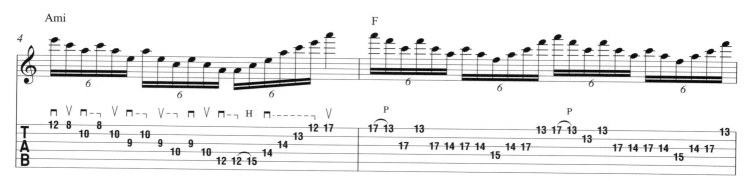

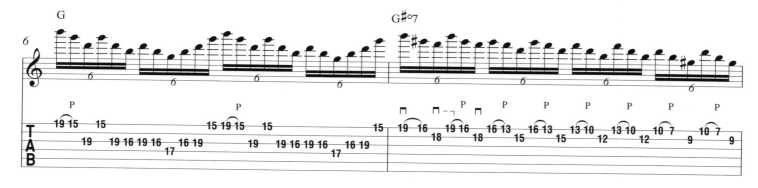

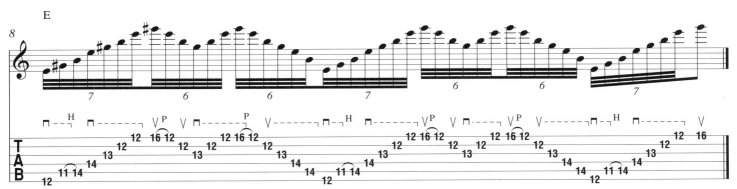

**FIG. 9.7.** "Hostile Takeover" (Intro)

Figure 9.8 is the arpeggio section from the track "Out For Blood" (*The Dark Lord Rises*, 2015). This arpeggio section is predominantly string skipping with some sweeping and single-note play towards the very end.

The section is in B minor. For the first ten bars, I'm playing a variation of the sixteenth-note base string-skipping lick featured earlier (figure 9.4). The picking patterns are notated below, but pretty much follows suit with figure 9.4, as far as the pick strokes and pull-offs are concerned.

The pattern moves through the chord sequence: Bmi F♯/A♯ (where I play A♯ diminished) A D G. It's all very straight ahead; I play one minor, one major, and one diminished triad string shape.

In bars 11 and 12, the chord goes to E minor, and here I play three- and five-string sweeps, once again using that figure-eight technique linking, combining, and connecting inversions.

In the final four bars, the chord changes to F♯, the V chord in B harmonic minor. For the first two beats, I play a lick I use quite frequently, combining a small three-string F♯ major triad arpeggio with a line from the scale. I sweep the small triadic shape and then alternate-pick the scale line (as shown). It's a very violinesque/Ritchie Blackmore type of neo-classical lick and works great with all types of triad/scale combinations.

After that two-beat lick, for the remainder of the last four bars of F♯ F♯/A♯, it's all *Hungarian minor*—a harmonic minor scale with a raised 4th degree. I play a short ascending passage for the last two beats of the first measure using some economy picking and then a lengthy descending Hungarian minor alternate-picked run to close out the arpeggio section. Hungarian minor has a very dark/evil distinct sound to it, and I use it all the time to create melodies as well in my soloing vocabulary.

# Out for Blood

Joe Stump

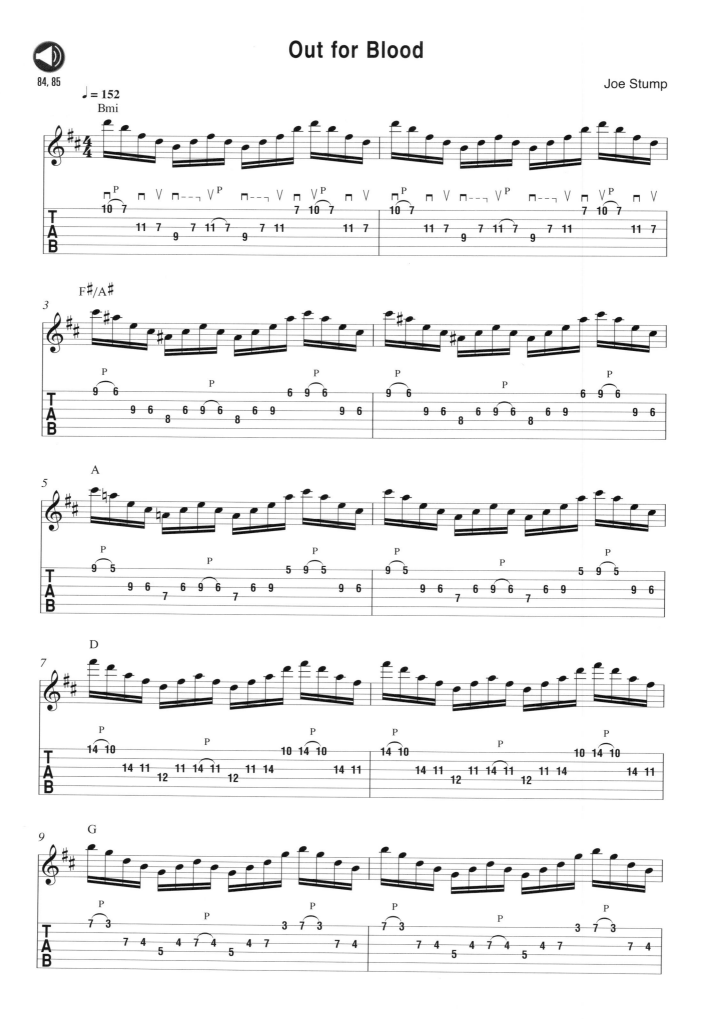

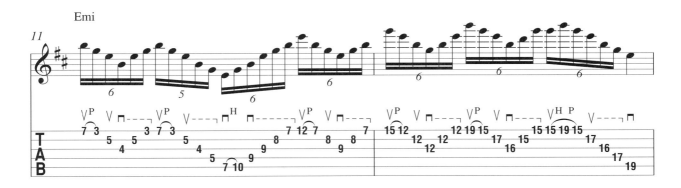

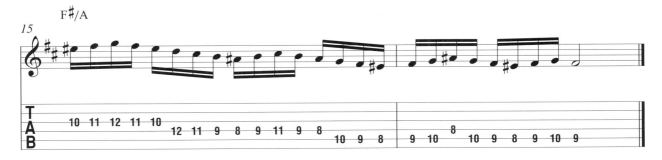

**FIG. 9.8.** "Out for Blood"

## CHAPTER 10

# Brothers in Shred

"Brothers in Shred" is the bonus track from my last solo record, *The Dark Lord Rises* (2015). It started out as an instructional piece that I gave to my students (and still is). I figured it'd be a cool thing to add on to the record. A couple friends guested on the track, hence the title.

Throughout the book, I've covered quite a few arpeggio studies/etudes as well as track excerpts. To finish, I figured it'd be a cool idea to feature an entire piece. The transcription is just about the entire track, with the exception of my main Phrygian dominant/double harmonic minor solo and my guests' solos. You have the riff/rhythm guitar intro, then the arpeggios played over the main chord sequence, and following that, a fairly lengthy solo section.

The track is a fast, double bass neo-classical/European power metal type of bit and starts out with the classic combination of diad and open-string riffing. (Again, *diads* are two-note chords, often associated with metal/hard rock riff/ rhythm guitar play.) The first section is in the key of A minor/harmonic minor. Therefore, I'm pedaling on the open A string with all of the two-note diad voicings contained on strings 3 and 4. It starts out with an A power chord, then on the last two beats of measure 1, I play a line inside the chords adding the 2nd degree of the scale, making it a sus2 voicing, then going to a full A minor where I'm playing the 5th and then the 3rd of the chord on strings 3 and 4. In measure 2, the chord changes to F, and I'm playing the root and 3rd. With any diad, you can play varying combinations of chord tones (root/3, 3/5, power chord with the 5 in the bass, 5/root, etc.). As the riff section continues, all of the diads are notated with their names above the voicings.

All of these diads are just smaller two-note portions of larger chord shapes, so in addition to internalizing these two-note, riff-oriented diads, it's also important to recognize the larger triadic shapes they stem from. Take note in the last two beats of measure 5, on the F and G major shapes, I'm playing the 3rd and 5th of both of those chords. (You don't always need the root in there to create the sound of the chord.) That diad is just a small two-string portion of the root/5 open C shape.

Along with the open string/diad riffing I'm also adding in single-note lines from the harmonic minor scale to connect the chords. (I'm using economy picking on that ascending three-note-per-string harmonic run in measure 6.)

The second part of the riff section is in the fifth mode of A harmonic minor: E Phrygian dominant. That scale goes by many names: Phrygian major, Spanish Phrygian, Gypsy minor, etc. When many flamenco guitarists (as well as European players) refer to Phrygian, they actually mean Phrygian dominant. The section opens with a descending scale run. On the lick, I'm alternate picking most of it, then using some pull-offs on the 4th string, which lets me play the 5th string on a down stroke. The riffing continues throughout the Phrygian section, this time pedaling on the low E with all of my diad voicings on strings 4 and 5. I play a combination root/3 and root/5 diads in the opening measure after the run.

In the third measure after the riff section, I'm once again using diads containing the 3/5 of the chord. This time, it's F major to E major with these originating from the larger open G shape from up at the nut. In the first ending of this section, I add in an ascending harmonic minor/diminished run (taking the G♯ diminished 7 arpeggio and adding the addition note from the harmonic minor scale) to connect back to the top of the riff section.

After the Phrygian section, it then goes to the chord progression that's used for the remaining portion of the piece. The combination of chords toggle between A natural and harmonic minor. Both the arpeggio and solo sections are played over these chords. This is one textbook example of how harmonic and natural minor are used together, as I'm playing arpeggios and single-note lines from both scales.

The arpeggio section starts with three-string sweeps. When I put this arpeggio study together, I wanted it to be useful to varying levels of players. If you're a fairly advanced metal player/shredder, it's an excellent way to memorize and internalize your shapes/inversions. If you're just getting started with sweep picking/arpeggio play, it shouldn't be all that intimidating (especially the three-string sections).

The three-string sweeps are played consistently in sextuplets the first two times through the chord progression, with the exception of that five-note diminished 7 figure over the E/G♯ played the second time through. I'm playing one sweep shape per bar, so it's easy to lock in and sync up (aside from the few diminished 7 shapes that are moved around in minor thirds). These first two times through work as an excellent inversion study, as the second time through the chord progression, I just play the next higher inversion of each arpeggio shape. The final time through the arpeggio section, the degree of technical difficulty raises significantly with various five- and three-string sweep combinations moving up and down the neck. By this time, you should be familiar with all of these shapes, as well as the picking patterns (shown). I can't stress enough how important it is to link the arpeggio shape to the larger triadic chordal shape it's derived from, and with the chord progression repeating several times, it'll certainly help reinforce that.

Note: In the complete audio file as well as the backing track to "Brothers in Shred," I've included the lengthy Phrygian solo section after the arpeggio section concludes. The Phrygian solo section is the only thing in the track not transcribed. I encourage you to create your own solo ideas, and improvise over this section.

86, 87

# Brothers in Shred

Joe Stump

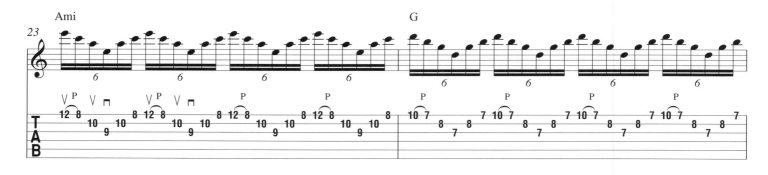

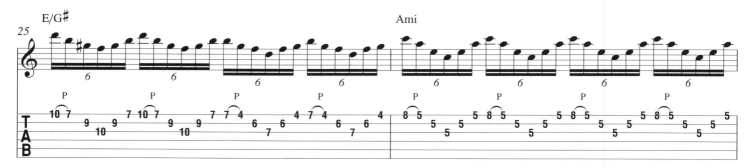

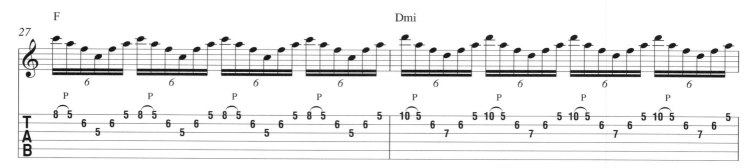

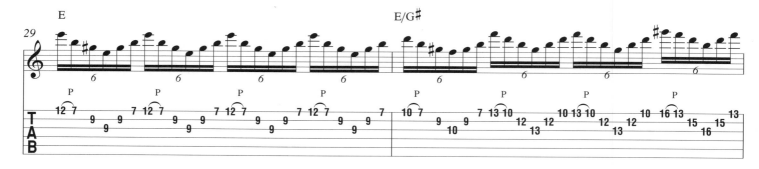

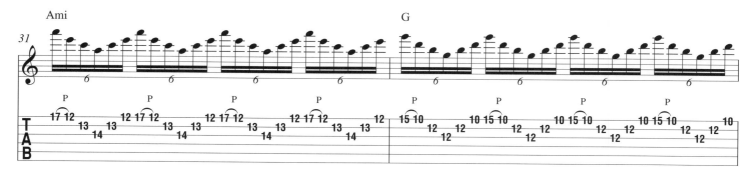

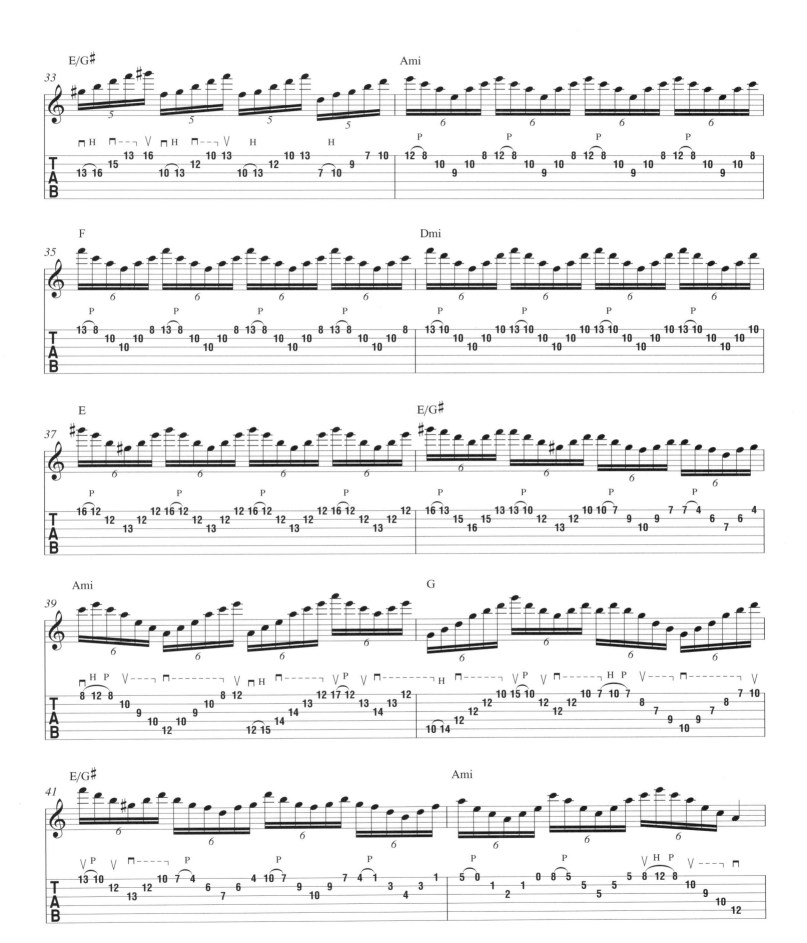

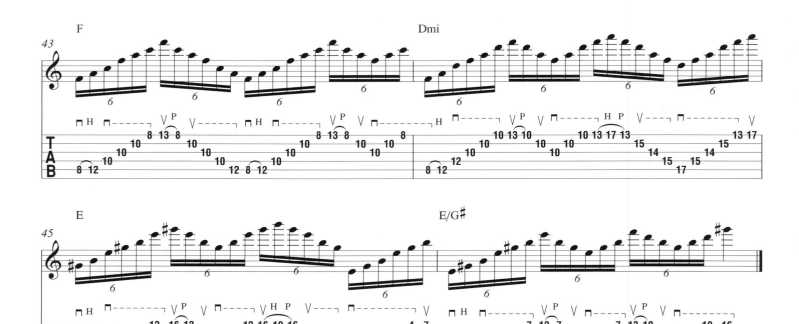

**FIG. 10.1.** "Brothers in Shred" Arpeggio Section

After the arpeggio section, the solo section begins. The solo contains many of the techniques that are a staple in this neo-classical/European shred style. Harmonic minor/diminished 7 runs, violin influenced mixed-minor runs, Baroque pedal tones, diatonic scale patterns, along with alternate and economy-picked passages are all contained here (with, of course, a few sweep arpeggios as well). Quite a few things to add to your solo vocabulary.

I start out with some note bending and phrasing. Then in bar 3 of the solo, I play a diminished 7 arpeggio run. Instead of playing the arpeggio in a sweep form, I'm playing it as a single-note line moving down in minor thirds (three frets at a time) across the strings. After the diminished line, I play an ascending harmonic/natural minor three-note-per-string run using economy picking, as the chord changes back to A minor. (Note: When learning this solo it's extremely important to pay attention to how the soloing ideas/techniques work with and over the chord progression.)

Over the F and D minor chords, it's more note bending and phrasing. Then when it goes to E and G# diminished 7, it's a signature Yngwie/Uli Jon Roth inspired Phrygian lick with the chord tones used as the target notes.

The second chorus of the solo starts in with a Bach/Malmsteen-inspired pedal-tone sequence, following suit with the chord changes. In this case, it's a pedal tone/pivot line where the line descends down the scale, and the note I'm pedaling off of/returning to is the highest pitch. As I said, the alternate-picked lines move down the scale with the chords, then resolve to A minor, using that classical arpeggio, adding the leading tone (7th degree of harmonic minor) and 2nd degree of the scale. Over the F and D minor, it's an alternate-/economy-picked scale fragment. Then the chorus closes out with a mixed minor violinesque run.

I use a diatonic four-note scale pattern to open the third time through the solo. I use the diatonic 4's (moving up or down the scale four notes at a time) quite a bit in my playing, and this particular melodic variation is very Ritchie Blackmore-inspired. Once again, the lick moves right along with the chord changes. I play a harmonic-minor melodic passage that resolves nicely back to the A minor chord. Over the F and D minor, I use an economy-picking lick. I'm quite fond of playing the scale three-notes-per-string and moving up in combinations of two and three strings.

On this lick, I'm using that standard three-note-per-string C major shape. I plug the picking pattern into the bottom four strings of the scale fingering and in the following measure, over the D minor, I repeat the same lick an octave higher. This section then ends with a combination of E major and G♯ diminished 7, three-string sweeps playing over the final two measures.

The final chorus starts out with my favorite lick in the solo, an extremely cool Blackmore-inspired old-school rock lick. Again, Ritchie Blackmore is one of my heroes and main influences. Mixing in this type of blues-based rock lick with dark classically influenced minor passages is something he'd do frequently. After the rock lick, it goes to a diminished run that then resolves to A minor. Note: In the diminished run, I'm just taking the G♯ diminished 7 arpeggio from the key and adding the middle tone of the scale to the three-note-per-string multi-octave run. Over the F and D minor, this time, I use a descending diatonic thirds pattern (i.e., I play a note from the scale and then the next lower note is two scale tones away). The solo section concludes with a descending harmonic minor run, alternate-picked across the strings (with the exception of the two areas when I'm sliding to the following note).

# Brothers in Shred

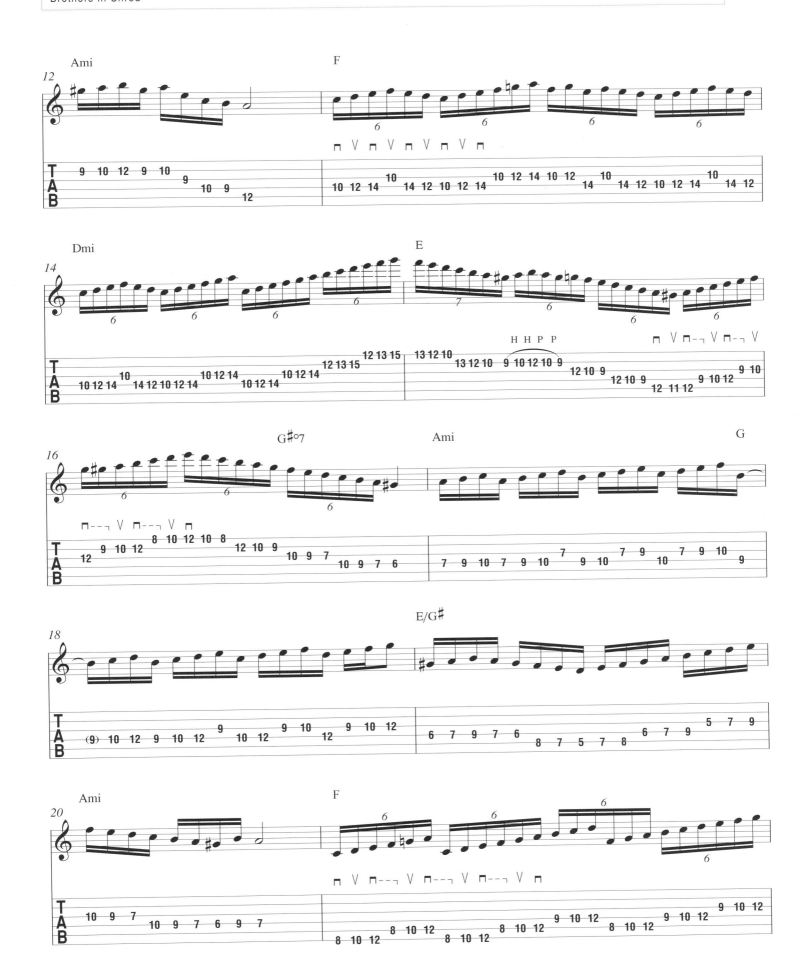

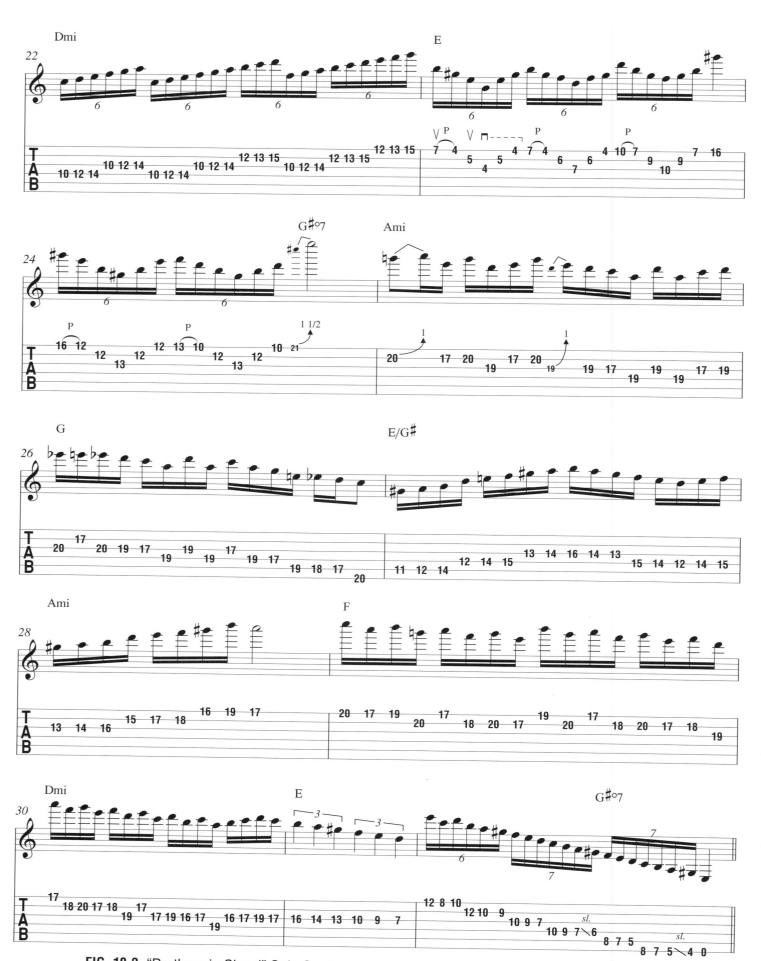

FIG. 10.2. "Brothers in Shred" Solo Section

## AFTERWORD

There you have it, quite a bit to work on in this final chapter as I've managed to combine riff/metal rhythm play with arpeggios and a multitude of solo ideas. Hopefully, working on these ideas will motivate you to explore the playing of the legendary European guitarists that inspired me and shaped my style; Ritchie Blackmore, Yngwie Malmsteen, Uli Jon Roth, Michael Schenker, and Gary Moore, as well as classical composers Bach, Vivaldi, Tchaikovsky, Paganini, Beethoven, and Mozart.

## ABOUT THE AUTHOR

Photo by Eddie Carlino, Bad Italian Productions

**Joe Stump** was named by *Guitar One* magazine as one of the top 10 fastest shredders of all time, by *Guitar World* as one of the 50 fastest players of all time, and by *Guitarist* magazine as one of the top 20 shredders of all time. He has appeared in countless guitar and metal-based publications, fanzines, and webzines worldwide. Referring to his specialty as "full throttle neo-classical shred/speed metal," Stump has toured the world both as a solo artist and with metal bands Joe Stump's Reign of Terror, HolyHell, RavenLord, and Exorcism. *The Dark Lord Rises* marks his tenth solo album. Stump has been the metal/shred guitar specialist at Berklee since 1993.

# More Fine Publications